Gift Aid item

Palestrina for All

Unwrapping, singing, celebrating

By
Jonathan Boswell

Copyright © 2018 by Jonathan Boswell

All rights reserved. No part of this publication may be reproduced, distributed or transmitted in any form or by any means, including photocopying, recording, or other electronic or mechanical methods, without the prior written permission of the publisher, except in the case of brief quotations embodied in critical reviews and certain other noncommercial uses permitted by copyright law.

Published by Jonathan Boswell
Production and distribution by eBookPartnership

ISBN: 978-1721968954

Palestrina in middle age, about to compose.

*Anonymous 16th century portrait
Courtesy of Biblioteca Casanatense, Roma*

Foreword

I first encountered Palestrina's music as a young man back in the 1950s. I listened so often to his Mass setting *Aeterna Christi Munera* that the vinyl record finally cracked. Many years later I sang enthusiastically in small choral groups devoted to early music. Palestrina's works, I found, provided a very good training ground for an amateur choral singer. I sang a fair amount of his music in workshops, sometimes in semi-concert conditions, and regularly for many years in church. Then I soaked myself in the relevant literatures. Wide ranging literature studies were familiar territory – as an academic general historian I had undertaken many of them.

I believe that Palestrina's music possesses not just a fascinating structure and style, and an exceptionally long, vividly eventful history, but also that it has a powerful ability to interact with emotion, imagination, social values, religious beliefs. Sadly, though, all sorts of barriers divide this music from the generality of music lovers today. It seemed to me that there was an overwhelming case for a new bridge, a fresh outreach. So I decided to write this book.

For several years I worked through most of the composer's huge opus and listened to all the recordings I could get my hands on, extracting large samples for the book. My descriptions in the book pay particular attention to texts, purposes and the total sound while addressing structure, style and voice deployment in accessible terms (expert musical knowledge is not assumed). There are chapters on

Palestrina's life and times, his music's changing fortunes over the centuries, and the viewpoints of its singers and conductors.

Palestrina's music poured out during the Catholic Counter Reformation of the late 16th century. Most of it is devoted to the Christian narrative and to Catholic beliefs and liturgy, while ideas about God echo throughout and relate to its essence. So whatever your beliefs, a fair understanding of these subjects is necessary. But the music's appeal and ongoing potential obviously go much wider. Secular and wide-ranging sorts of response to it - emotional, spiritual and imaginative - form a central focus of the book.

I am grateful to the people I have sung Palestrina with over the years, too many to mention here. Helpful thoughts came from Joseph Angolano, the Rev David Brown, Johan Herczog, Jill Mitchell, Eoghain Murphy, John Piper, Michael Procter, Ciro Quaranta, Hugh Rosenbaum, David Salvage, Yaron Shavit, Martin Stacey and Dominic White OP. Advice on historical aspects and specialist sources came from Simon Ditchfield, Rev Dermot Fenlon, James Garratt, Thomas Muir and John O'Malley SJ. Andrew Wilton and Sophie Boswell commented on aspects of readability. I am grateful to Peter Wilson for knowledgeable help on a range of technical issues. Ian Henghes provided valuable assistance at the final compilation stage. eBookPartnership have been very efficient in organising and producing both print and ebook versions, and thanks are particularly due to Chantal Chevalier for her help through most of the process.

Special thanks are due to Professor Giancarlo Rostirolla, longtime Palestrina expert and Artistic Director of the Fondazione Giovanni Pierluigi da Palestrina, for help in Rome and for arranging access to the Centro di Studi Palestriniani in the *citta* Palestrina, with its indispensable collection of books, monographs, records of seminars and conferences, and bibliographical sources. Helpful advice on illustrations came from the Accademia di Santa Cecilia.

A key part was played by interviews with choral conductors: David Allinson, Martin Baker, Stephen Darlington, Alistair Dixon, Blanaid Murphy, James O'Donnell, Patrick Russill, Bruno Turner, and Terry Worroll. Peter Phillips kindly provided illuminating reminiscences on the role of Palestrina's music in the early days of the Tallis Scholars. Andrew Carwood was a great stimulus during a memorable week of singing efforts under his direction in Triora, Liguria, and in subsequent discussion.

I owe a great debt to Noel O'Regan for generously sharing his exceptional knowledge of the composer and for commenting in detail on a complete early draft of the book, and to Claude Crozet for many helpful discussions.

As with much previous writing my wife Jill helped at every stage with copy editing and stylistic issues. None of these individuals should be held responsible for judgements in this book or for any faults and errors which are entirely my own.

Jonathan Boswell
Spring 2018

Table of Contents

Foreword

Chapter 1	Prince of Music ?	1
Chapter 2	Palestrina in his own time	15
Chapter 3	Love poetry and devotional diversities	29
Chapter 4	Sorrow, suffering, hope and glory	49
Chapter 5	A music of amity and ideal community	67
Chapter 6	'The quality of mercy': *Kyrie eleison*	79
Chapter 7	*Gloria* and *Credo*	95
Chapter 8	Controversies, choirs, conductors	109
Chapter 9	Sounding the mystery: *Sanctus* and *Benedictus*	125
Chapter 10	Peace and eternity: *Agnus Dei*	139

Select bibliography ... 159

Index of works referrred to ... 163

Chapter 1

Prince of Music ?

Giovanni Pierluigi da Palestrina (1524/5-1594), a towering figure in Western music, was remarkably productive. His hundreds of works engaged with wide varieties of poetic, scriptural and liturgical texts. He was highly successful in his own time, living and working in the Rome of the Counter Reformation or Catholic Reform. His music carried previous centuries of musical evolution to a culminating synthesis, a peak point in choral music, often labelled as an *ars perfecta*. A highly eventful reception and discussion history followed, focussing many inexorable and perennial issues about music, its cultural influence and complex meanings.

Although Palestrina composed many secular works, the bulk of his output was devoted to the Christian narrative, and to worship inside the Catholic Church. There is virtually no scriptural or other source in the Church's liturgy which he fails at some point to address. Sections of the 150 Old Testament psalms feature in hundreds of his works. From the Old Testament he also sets the *Lamentations of Jeremiah* and the erotic-cum-spiritual *Song of Songs*. He engages extensively with the Church's hymns and antiphons, also drawing on medieval religious lyrics. Among works securely attributed to him are some 330 sacred motets, 68 offertories, 35

Magnificats, 72 hymns, and 49 sacred madrigals. His coverage of the Church's Year includes all its seasons and major feasts.

What stands out most, however, is Palestrina's engagement a mighty 104 times over with the six sections of the regular Mass commonly set to music: *Kyrie eleison, Gloria, Credo, Sanctus, Benedictus* and *Agnus Dei.* The 104 appears to be a record number. It is an historic record for settings of a single set of texts by any Western composer, religious or secular, a concentration aptly characterised as 'telling', even 'mind boggling' (1). J.S. Bach composed over 200 church cantatas, a massive achievement but hardly comparable since these were framed around highly diverse religious texts. Among Palestrina's near contemporaries the fertile, influential Orlando di Lasso seems to have composed about 60 Mass settings. The Catholic composers Thomas Tallis and William Byrd, who faced daunting problems in post-Reformation England, each appears responsible for only three Mass settings. 22 Masses came from Tomas Luis de Victoria, priest *cum* composer and less long-lived than Palestrina, 19 from another leading Spanish composer, Francisco Guerrero.

A tribute alike to the voracious appetite of the Catholic world for Masses and to Palestrina's long service of the Church, the consequences were mixed. So many settings would make it hard to choose later on which ones to perform, resulting in a tendency over the centuries to stick conservatively to a familiar few. The varied texts and spiritually intense phases of the choral Mass allowed for a lot of compositional freedom. Two long, highly detailed texts would be problematic for a composer, the *Gloria* and more particularly the *Credo.* But the lesser 'wordiness' of the other sections would give ample scope for the music to move more freely towards meditation, jubilation or rhapsody.

In the 19th century it became fashionable to idealise Palestrina as the saviour of church music at the time of the Counter Reformation when its more intricate art forms in the Church appeared to come under serious threat. He was viewed as a leading papal favourite, a supreme Catholic and/or pan-Christian composer, his music eulogised for its 'purity' and 'spirituality'. He was also regarded as the supreme maestro of vocal polyphony and sheer compositional excellence in counterpoint, a textbook paragon. Often these images overlapped. Romanticisation would reach a climax in Hans Pfitzner's opera *Palestrina* first performed in 1917. This cast the composer as a sort of musical saint, with his celebrated *Missa Papae Marcelli* dictated by angels.

The hype was excessive and painstaking academic work, which started in a small way in the early 1800s, would be needed to redress it. Two comprehensive editions of the works eventually appeared, the work of musicologists Gustav Haberl and Raffaele Casimiri, both published over long periods (2). Surprisingly, some additional works would be discovered as late as in 1950. Data about Palestrina's life and work have been researched to the point of apparent exhaustion, while technical analysis of his works continues to fascinate specialist musicologists.

A sense has developed of Palestrina's music as dry, erudite, remote. Legend, stereotype and church neglect have all contributed to this, also historicist pigeon-holing and academic specialisation. For many generations the music has been used as a dry-as-dust learning exercise for music students. Contrary to an image of Palestrina as a creature of romantic myth, it is an austerely technical, recondite treatment which has largely dominated the literature in recent times, with the bibliographies listing hundreds of articles and reviews in academic journals.

LISTENING TO THE TOTAL SOUND

First, a word of advice to my readers. A key way to engage with Palestrina's music applies whether you are familiar with it, or a complete newcomer, or have already had a taste of Palestrina and would like to try some more. Here is my advice. Take advantage of the spate of high quality recordings which have emerged since the 1980s. These have come from some of the best national and international choral groups, including leading chamber, cathedral and college chapel choirs. Find a few of these recordings, relax and listen to the total sound.

A good starting-point would be the celebrated *Missa Papae Marcelli*, focussing on its *Kyrie eleison* section. An alternative would be the less familiar *Missa O Rex Gloriae,* ideally its three last sections, *Sanctus, Benedictus* and *Agnus Dei.* The latter are moderate in length, amounting to about seven minutes listening.

Listen several times. Try to lay aside preconceptions. As far as possible avoid thinking about the text, the history or the purposes of the music, let alone its structure. This may be difficult if you know Latin, harder if you are familiar with the make-up of 16th century counterpoint or with musical structures in general. It will be harder still if you have a highbrow prejudice against unstructured listening. Instead, aim to give yourself unconditionally to the total sound. After all, this is how most people will first experience the music, and it can produce rich rewards.

Allow space in your mind for an immediate spontaneous response. What sort of music is this ? What physical effects does it induce, what random emotions or wider thoughts ? Steady movement towards ever receding horizons ? A boat floating serenely over the waves ? Colours or shapes of natural life or landscapes, maybe abstract art or architectural forms ? What do the harmonious relationships between the different voice parts suggest to you ?

An immediate impression is of a sort of chamber music involving not instruments but people, the singers, who are communicating directly or 'conversationally'. We become aware of varied minglings of voices. Their exchanges seem somehow rounded and balanced. One or other voice part may be emphasised but is never completely in charge. Hardly ever is any part isolated but neither is it swallowed up. Nearly always the parts are reciprocating and interweaving. There is a lack of obvious tension. The tone is temperate, the pace insistent but gentle.

There are also puzzles, however. The music seems to elude the clear-cut major/minor contrasts, the counter-moves between 'happy' and 'sad', things we normally find in the tonal system within conventional 'classical', 'romantic' or 'popular' musics. We are likely to miss a sense of moving clearly from conflict to resolution. It is tempting to ask, is this music ingenuously simple or ingeniously complex ? Is its complexity largely hidden ? Does it speak confidently or with a touch of reserve, even of agnostic unknowing? Its continuity seems baffling. At the start it steals upon us, at the end it seems to leave us in suspense.

Palestrina's music is mostly *contrapuntal*. Typically it introduces a melodic line which then goes through intricate mutations as it gets taken up successively by the different voice parts. Sometimes the original melodic line is precisely imitated, more often it gets altered. A simple example is shown below, the opening phrases of a motet *Dilectus meus descendit in hortum,* 'My beloved goes down to his garden'. The plangent melodic lead on *dilectus meus,* which seems to express the lover's yearning, is initiated by the cantus singers at point 1, then taken up by the first altos (point 2), the basses (3), the second altos (4), the tenors (5), and again by the cantus (6): examples of precise imitation. Then comes a touch of 'pictorialism': Palestrina sets the words *descendit in hortum* on a downward melodic line, mostly varied between the voices. Notice a familiar feature in Palestrina which tends towards rhythmic freedom within a steady pulse. Voice part entries occur on the beat at points 1, 2 and 6 but occur off-beat at points 3, 4 and 5.

6   Palestrina For All

Two provisos are necessary. First, Palestrina's counterpoint is not always structured around a few clearly defined melodic leads as here. Much of his follow-up material and sometimes whole works are more pluralistic, relying on simultaneities or greater diversities of melodic lines. Second, not all of his music is contrapuntal. He also makes use of homophony where the voice parts bunch together in chords. Such chordal episodes go well with certain words or ideas as well as helping to provide variety. Very occasionally a piece is almost entirely chordal, while a very few of his works are *polychoral*, i.e. designed for two or more choirs (eight or more parts), where a lot of homophony becomes both necessary and effective.

The music is corporate yet pluralistic. It is highly communal while avoiding a parts-to-whole subordination or tight collectivism. Hardly at all will the altos, tenors, basses or top part or *cantus* be singing separately (3). Yet each part tends to have its own entries and exits, along with ample shares of differentiation and things which are nice to sing.

A key feature is *consonance*. By the late 16th century, when Palestrina was composing, complex rules or conventions were needed to make this work (4). We need to bear in mind that 'consonance' is not an absolute phenomenon but a concept which varies between musical cultures in different parts of the world, and between periods. Today's listeners can readily hear Palestrina's music as harmonious. In fact, it makes some use of dissonance but with great restraint. Also recognisable is a 'folk music', diatonic sort of sound, reflecting a prevalence of white notes, an extreme scarcity of sharps and flats.

RELIGIOUS INTENSITY, DIVERSIFIED OUTREACH

The religious dimension in Palestrina's music has been stereotyped. One approach has been clannish and exclusivist, treating his music virtually as the property of the Catholic Church and its liturgy. Another stereotype views the music as intriguing and beautiful but essentially a museum piece, a relic of a far distant religion and culture.

In his *Oxford History of Western Music* Richard Taruskin colourfully expresses the latter view. Hypothesising a poignant end to the Palestrina story, he portrays the music as culmination of a long evolving musical style but in this sense as two-edged: fascinating and glorious, yes, but vulnerable to a bitter-sweet sort of remoteness or isolatedness, 'the beauty and despair of the *ars perfecta*'. It would arrive at an end-point, a cul-de-sac, a sort of mummified status. 'Everything perfect, in this world, is doomed' …'The only way to preserve the perfected art was to seal it off from history …freezing the perfect polyphonic art of Palestrina into a timeless dogma, as it were, to join the timeless dogmas of theology', so that it became 'timelessly embalmed'. Palestrina's music 'had in effect stepped out of history and into eternity' with the result that 'the *ars perfecta* …still exists but not in a way that matters any more' (5).

Historically, this view is bizarre. Evidence suggests that some musical genres have a strong cyclical or survivor quality, repeating phases of disuse or neglect, then resurgence. It is true that for two centuries or more the performance of Palestrina's music would largely rely on life support from the papacy while active interest would be limited to a tiny elite of music historians or theorists. However, the music would 're-enter' history substantively in four main ways: *first*, a 19th century Palestrina revival involving leading composers and music lovers; *second*, a modest revival inside the Catholic Church; *third*, a significant ongoing place within the choral singing community and the early music movement; and *fourth*, a spate of brilliant recordings since the 1980s.

The view that Palestrina's music is 'doomed' through its close servicing of 'dogma', and 'theology', things described as 'not mattering any more', is biased and contestable. However, it has the merit at least of drawing attention to a linkage which needs to be considered carefully.

Palestrina's music is indeed steeped in European Christianity. It inherits much basic material from centuries of plainchant as regularly sung in monasteries, convents and basilicas. For long periods its survival would depend on church patronage within rituals saturated with ideas of mystery, ultimacy and a specially present God. Its liturgical role continues, as do religious responses matching in variety and potential an exceptional coverage of Christian beliefs. As pertinent as ever, therefore, are criteria relating to the music's blend with church liturgy, its treatment of the Christian narrative, and how it can intimate something of the nature of the infinite, merciful, trinitarian God that Christians believe in.

This raises an issue over 'bridging the gap' between Christian listeners and those outside the churches who may enjoy the music at least as much. How to address the fact that many (probably most) of the music's present day admirers do not subscribe to its religiousness ?

Some leading commentators have shed light on the issue. Michael Tippett associated great music in general with 'a touch of the everlasting', Ralph Vaughan Williams viewed it as a quest for 'ultimate realities …through the medium of beauty'. John Eliot Gardiner confessed that although an agnostic he 'feels like a Christian' when conducting the great religious works of J.S. Bach. The philosopher Charles Taylor discusses how 'free-wheelers' in a secular age, vaguely in search of 'something more', can experience 'a kind of undefined spirituality' in 'Absolute' music as 'being moved by what is powerful and deep, but not needing to know where this is to be found, whether in heaven or on earth or in the depths of our own being – or even whether these alternatives are exclusive' (6).

That Palestrina's music reverberates multi-dimensionally for different categories of people is a consistent theme in this book. The rich inspiration it can provide for Christians and other theists will emerge repeatedly. But for all its deep religiousness it is not pressuring or 'pushy'. Amateur singers warm to it as respecting their natural vocal ranges, letting their voices float free and undiluted, enhancing their roles in small ensembles. Historically, responses to the music have been richly diverse and this continues. Emotion, memories, aspirations, thoughts of material objects or abstract ideas all form part of the mix. One way of understanding and hearing relates to social relationships and community. I am going to claim that Palestrina's counterpoint offers a form of social symbolism, that it intimates the essence of communicating well, 'good conversation', relationships of fraternity and cooperation, 'ideal community'.

STRUCTURE OF THE BOOK

With an opus running to hundreds of works, it was difficult to decide which ones to focus on. Very large numbers of vocal scores in the comprehensive editions had to be scanned. The likely availability of recordings had to be checked (why discuss works which readers would be unable to access ?). I listened repeatedly. I pursued some relatively neglected works. Finally came judgements as to representativeness, significant contrasts and overall quality of both works and recordings. In this last respect, of course, personal preferences are unavoidable, and I realise that not everyone will agree with my choices or interpretations.

Selection was most difficult in the case of Palestrina's upwards of 400 motets and many other works, since only small proportions of these have been recorded. I arrived at a sample of over 80, of which 45 are referred to in the text. The 104 securely attributed Mass settings were more straightforward. I briefly scanned 95. The number finally qualifying for my core sample, for purposes of more detailed examination, was 32 or about 30 % of the total.

I avoid too many technical terms while steering clear of abstruse issues such as the use of this or that traditional church mode or the distant, often speculative origins of lead melodies. I use footnotes very sparingly. The expert musicology surrounding Palestrina is extensive but also concentrated, and there is wide scholarly agreement on the provenance, style and structure of his music. Rather than cite such sources in detail in the main body of the text I thought it best to provide a select bibliography.

Chapter 2 portrays Palestrina's career and life story while also sketching the context of late 16th century Rome as directly or indirectly influencing his work. Chapter 3 further discusses different ways of listening. It samples Palestrina's music through his settings of love poetry, notably the erotic-cum-sacred *Song of Songs*, then through diverse devotional purposes up to some outstanding works at the start of the Church's Year at Advent and Christmas.

Chapter 4 follows the music through the seasons of Lent, Easter and the rest of the Christian narrative and the Church Year, with their themes of sorrow, suffering, triumph and glory, and underlying all of these, a sense of mystery. By this point we are able to venture on a provisional view of the structure and style of the music, on how it synthesises features leading to stability, balance and fluidity.

Chapter 5 considers a challenging general issue. Palestrina's music adheres to certain practices as between the voice parts: individual differentiation of melodic lines, broadly equal participation, consonance, and graceful forms of mutuality. I suggest that this combination has socio-symbolic significance. It can be interpreted as connoting good human relationships, optimum mutual communication or 'ideal community'. Other Renaissance composers do this too but less consistently and over a smaller canvas.

Further general issues are addressed in chapter 8. This glances at the reception history, particularly the 19th century revival and the music's changing fortunes within the Catholic Church up to recent times. It looks at problems and different styles of performance, drawing on the 'frontline' viewpoints of choir directors, church musicians and singers.

The remainder of the book is devoted to Palestrina's Mass settings, addressing their successive sections in separate chapters. Chapter 6 addresses the *Kyrie eleison*, chapter 7 the *Gloria* and *Credo*, chapter 9 the *Sanctus* and *Benedictus*, and chapter 10 the *Agnus Dei*. This differs from previous treatments. I believe it reflects the particular importance of the Masses. My aim is to bring out the changes or continuities of text, liturgical role, style and structure, and the diverse forms of emotional, spiritual and imaginative response that each section opens up.

Footnotes

(1) Richard Taruskin, *The Oxford History of Western Music, volume 1*, Oxford 2010, 632.

(2) Franz Xavier Haberl and others, *Ioannis Petraloysii Praenestini Opera Omnia*, volumes 1-33, Breitkopf and Hartel, Leipzig 1862-1907. Raffaele Casimiri and others, *Le Opere Complete di Giovanni Pierluigi da Palestrina*, volumes 1-35, Fratelli Scalera, Rome 1939-1999.

(3) The traditional term *cantus* for the highest voice part is fairly standard in printed vocal scores, and simpler than having to indicate repeatedly the alternatives of treble or soprano.

(4) In Western Europe, broadly from the 14th century onwards, *contrapunctus* was taken to mean a form of polyphony (the sounding of several musical lines simultaneously) aiming at a balance between 'consonance' and 'dissonance' in favour of the former. By Palestrina's time ideas of consonance had evolved considerably. Exposed intervals of a fourth had retreated while thirds were preferred. More voice parts were entering the mix. Whereas in earlier phases there were only two (the principal line, usually tenor or *cantus fermus*, and the contra-tenor), the vocal parts had typically expanded to four: *cantus*, alto, tenor and bass.

(5) Richard Taruskin, see 1 above, pages 629-30.

(6) Michael Tippett, *Moving into Aquarius,* Routledge, London, 1959, Paladin Books, 1974, 18, 22. Ralph Vaughan Williams, cited in James Day, *Vaughan Williams*, Oxford, 1998, 103. John Eliot Gardiner in 'Bach', a special issue, *The Guardian* 12 December 2005. Charles Taylor, *A Secular Age*, Harvard 2007, 359-60.

Chapter 2

Palestrina In His Own Time

Giovanni Pierluigi Praenestina was born in 1525 or 1526 in Palestrina, a small hill town in the *campagna* about thirty miles from Rome – after which he was later called Giovanni Pierluigi *da* Palestrina. Historically, the citizens of Palestrina have been proud of its status as a *citta,* its cathedral and its interesting Roman remains. The composer's birthplace in the town centre forms part of the Fondazione Giovanni Pierluigi da Palestrina, devoted to his works and legacy, and a gracefully idealised statue of him adorns the town's main piazza.

Palestrina's family were middle class, small landowners or business folk. At a young age he became a choirboy in the town's small cathedral, San Agapito and showed talent in this role. He was soon recruited, still as a boy, to sing in the choir school at the historic Roman basilica of Santa Maria Maggiore. A life changing impact is likely to have come from the choral music at the basilica, along with the building's high traditions and lofty architecture, and more generally from the exciting environment of Rome. His training there led to further music studies. Then in 1547, on returning to Palestrina, Giovanni Pierluigi became organist and choirmaster at

San Agapito. He married a young woman from a local family, Lucrezia Gori, and they had three sons.

After 1551 Palestrina spent his entire career in Rome. Through long phases he was master of music at three historic basilicas: St Peter's, San Giovanni Laterano and Santa Maria Maggiore. From the 1560s he held the prestigious title of composer to the papal chapel, fairly soon reaching a position of remarkable musical ascendancy in Rome, at the centre of the Catholic Church.

Palestrina's early career in Rome brought dramatic ups-and-downs. Favoured by one pope, he was catapulted into membership of the ultra-prestigious, sometimes fractious Sistine Chapel choir with mixed results. *Dis*favoured by another pope on account of being a married member of that choir, he was dismissed from it, albeit with a reasonable pension. Following a dispute with senior clergy over funding issues, he later resigned as *maestro* at the Lateran basilica. Palestrina clearly had a high view of his talent and status, and, in all likelihood, something of a temper.

By the 1560s leading currents of official opinion in the Church would be crucial for him. As part of the Catholic Reform or Counter Reformation - alongside major changes in church practice, organisation and strategy - top circles in and around the Vatican had serious anxieties about church music. Much of it had become too drawn-out, elaborate and showy, cluttered by excessive ornament and unrecognisable texts. Many saw it as tainted by secularism and impurity. At a critical time for the Church, surely it should be geared to represent Catholic doctrine and ethics, shaped so as to attract and hold the people ? Contrary to some later stereotypes, an urge to simplify and purify church music did not feature in the official decrees of the Church's official reform programme, the Council of Trent. What did appear in the Council's final decrees in 1562 were, first, a delegation of responsibility for music to local echelons in the church (recognising implicitly that it was likely to remain diverse in practice), and, second, a strong desire for it to be clearly differentiated from secular music, excluding things that were 'lascivious or impure' (1).

Some of this was unrealistic. To exclude secular tunes completely was hardly practicable since 'sacred' and 'secular' could be hard to distinguish. Popular tunes, even some rowdy or outright bawdy ones, would continue to feature in church music, including in Palestrina's, albeit dignified (and easier to disguise) by way of longer note values, steadier rhythms or subtle variations. However, the Council's desire for some qualitative difference had more to be said for it. There has always been a case for church music to stand out from everyday kinds. At the time there was certainly a need for less clutter and for the texts to be heard more clearly. On the other hand, such an aim could easily overshoot, producing banal or mechanical results, even threatening the basics of choral polyphony.

The idea that the church authorities had a Damascene moment after hearing a single Palestrina work, the famous *Missa Papae Marcelli,* impressed by its clear rendering of the text and its beauty, is simplistic. What is true is that on a narrow interpretation of 'clarity' and 'intelligibility' he could have produced a minimalist solution like that of Vincenzo Ruffo, an ultra-conformist contemporary. Questionably assuming that even in regular parts of the Mass every single word needed to sound out clearly, Palestrina could have gone for chord-after-chord music, nailing each syllable down to a single sound, a bleak approach being adopted by Calvinist music (though generally avoided in Lutheran Germany and Elizabethan England). This would have destroyed a rich musical legacy. The loss of melodic multilinearity and interweaving voice parts would doubtless have made him weep.

Instead he made some not-too-onerous concessions. He refined and intensified certain features already evident in his liturgical compositions: on the one hand, a style regarded as noble, solemn and devout, and on the other, a degree of clarity sufficient for the text to sound out clearly.

MIDDLE YEARS AND A TRAUMATIC CRISIS

Palestrina did so well in Rome over many years that it would become hard to leave. By and large it was a good place to live in. The cosmopolitan atmosphere and a plurality of church potentates and institutions made for a wide circle of patronage, whereas dependence on a single secular ruler would have been constraining, while staying put was good for family ties and stability of career. So when prestigious princely offers came, as they did from Vienna in 1568 and Mantua in 1583 (in the latter case at his own instance), Palestrina held out for hefty increases in salary. Did this simply reflect a high view of his own worth ? Was he serious about moving ? Surely he must have thought refusal all too likely ? We cannot be sure, but a gut preference for life and work in Rome was probably the strongest factor.

Palestrina took care to keep in with powerful patrons. He worked for some years for the wealthy, worldly Cardinal Ippolito d'Este and would correspond with a highly cultured, well connected prince, Duke Guglielmo Gonzaga of Mantua (see chapter 7). We know hardly anything about his family, friendships or professional relationships. Among contemporaries he would have known quite well were Giovanni Animuccia, a leading singer and composer, and the brilliant Spanish priest-composer Tomas Luis de Victoria. Victoria may well have been his student for a while and they seem to have influenced each other's music.

The years 1572-80 brought major tragedies. In Rome there were phases of plague and famine partly related to war. Family deaths had to be endured. In 1572 Palestrina's eldest son Rodolfo, a promising young musician, died of the plague. In 1573 he lost a brother, Silla. A further blow followed in 1575 with the death, shortly after marrying, of his second son Angelo. This left only a third son, Iginio. Palestrina's composing appears to have suffered during this period, and nothing was published between 1575 and 1581.

The most serious blow came in late 1580 when his wife Lucrezia died of an epidemic. Clearly this tragedy was the worst, and a series of dramatic events quickly followed. Almost immediately Giovanni Pierluigi petitioned the pope, moved *ex devotione zelo et fervore*, for consent to become a priest. His request was fast-forwarded. In a striking sign of top-level support Pope Gregory X111 issued a brief 'to our beloved son, Joannes Petraloysius', decreeing that he could indeed be ordained priest and granting him a permanent clerical position at the basilica of Santa Maria Maggiore with nil or minimal duties and a small salary.

In December 1580 Palestrina duly received the clerical tonsure. In the normal course he would then have prepared for minor orders, leading eventually to ordination as sub-deacon, deacon and finally priest. But a surprise move came a few weeks later, only eight months after Lucrezia's death and three months after receiving the clerical tonsure. He abandoned the aspiration to be a priest. Speedily and quietly, he celebrated marriage to a widow probably in her late thirties, Virginia Dormoli.

Clearly, Giovanni Pierluigi had gone through a traumatic phase. It seems likely he would turn to God: prayer, reflection and spiritual counselling would be important (for his religiousness see later). He may have contemplated giving up composing (something Pope Gregory was clearly against), although the priesthood would not necessarily enforce such a step. It is possible that advice came from Philip Neri, a charismatic spiritual figure and sought-after counsellor in Rome, later canonised, whom Palestrina would have known. In the end a renewed sense of music as his inescapable vocation, its pursuit seemingly easier as a layman, was probably decisive.

It also seems reasonable to assume that after many years of married life Giovanni Pierluigi felt that he needed a wife. Virginia had inherited a small, lucrative skin and fur business from her first husband, leading some later commentators to describe her simply as 'a rich widow', implying that this was the central reason for the marriage. This seems rather insulting to both of them. The business would indeed prove helpful during Palestrina's last period, invaluable in expanding publication of his works. But alongside the financial and career motives, the possibility of mutual attraction must be allowed for, and a hope for companionship and comfort seems likely.

LATE 16TH CENTURY ROME

Rome in Palestrina's time was a city of extreme, even violent contrasts. When the popes were not engaging in solemn liturgy or private devotion, they were governing often with a repressive hand, conducting European diplomacy, battling against Protestantism or the Turks, promoting Counter Reformation programmes to cleanse and update the Church. Beggars crowded the city. Papal discipline was usually ineffective in the face of widespread crime and a large red-light district housing thousands of prostitutes. Periodic attacks of the plague, rival gangs in the streets and bouts of turbulence in the outlying papal states often made for a sense of insecurity.

Within the papal court cardinal nephews and favourites still accumulated power and wealth, though the worst scandals of some notorious earlier papacies had receded. The courts of the leading cardinals, some of them scions of leading Italian dynasties, the d'Este, Farnese, Medici or Gonzaga, featured cultural patronage and lavish display. The rival great powers of Catholic Europe, Spain, Austria and France, were constantly intriguing for influence, particularly during the politically fraught conclaves to elect new popes.

The Catholic Reform was having varied impacts. Patterns of repentance, reparation and change of life co-existed with luxury and pride, often within the same individuals. Religious confraternities old and new were drawing many people into regular routines of prayer, abstinence, attendance at Mass, care of pilgrims, charitable social work. Devotion to Christ brought hundreds of members of the new religious orders into the hospitals, orphanages and streets to provide food, clothing and help to the sick and the poor. Through the year elaborate ceremonies marked the great feasts of the Church, with large influxes of pilgrims crowding in from across Europe and beyond.

The ritual practices of Catholicism were in full spate. In a eulogistic book *Roma Sancta* (1578) the exiled English don and priest Gregory Martin listed candles, crosses, banners, flowers, window hangings; 'the shewing of relikes'; 'lampes alwaies burning'; rich vestments; 'a rich canopee' over the tabernacle. He remarked on large amounts of preaching, including to the Jews, annually commandeered in from their 'synagog' and 'streate', on the penitential element in Holy Week (the *flagellanti* and whipcords), and on charitable work. Symbolic physical movement was important: solemn processions inside and outside church, candle holding, fingering of rosaries, 'the Holy Stayers' at the Laterano with people mounting on their knees and kissing the Cross; the 'standing, kneeling, capping, crossing' during Mass. Lots of music too: 'every Companie with their great quyer singing all the way', the pope's choir singing 'with most excellent melodies', and 'a new musicke of the best', doubtless including Palestrina's (2).

Further inspiration came literally from underground. Many of the catacombs, the remains of early Christian worship and burial in ancient Rome, were being opened up and celebrated. A Paleo-Christian revival movement was under way. Philip Neri had undertaken night visits to the catacombs for prayer and meditation soon after his arrival in Rome in 1533, and this practice grew thereafter under his aegis. Excavation of the sacred underground reached an excited climax in 1578 with the rediscovery of the so-called Catacombs of Saint Priscilla, engendering a feeling summed up by the contemporary church historian Cesare Baronio.

> 'We can find no better words to describe its extent and its many corridors than to call it a subterranean city …. All Rome was filled with wonder, for it had no idea that in its neighbourhood there was a hidden city, filled with tombs from the persecution of the Christians' .

The holy 'subterranean city' was interpreted as further validating Rome's claims to primacy as founding rock of the Church. It provided an additional incentive for the pilgrimage to Rome, a source of relics for altars, and a sense of help from the prayers of numerous anonymous as well as identifiable martyred saints. Indeed the theme of martyrdom was very much alive. New martyrs were being mourned and celebrated as Catholic missionaries met with persecution and death in various parts of the world. In the church of San Tommaso di Canterbury, a homing centre for English Catholics in Rome, whenever news came through of another missionary martyred in Protestant Elizabethan England, prayers were said and a solemn *Te Deum* sung.

The writer Michel de Montaigne, who spent several months in Rome in 1580-81, was full of lively observations. Himself an observant Catholic, he suspected that the Romans were less devout than the French, referring drily to 'ecclesiastical idleness'. He appreciated the fervent ceremonies, 'many excellent sermons', the Jesuit mission against 'the heretics of our time', 'a great many private devotions and brotherhoods in which many evidences of piety are seen', and the presence of Pope Gregory X111, 'a handsome old man' (still with a Bolognese accent) whose handling of the papal role he thought impressive. He also expanded on the public executions, the red-light districts, the men's sober clothing, the women's greater freedom in public places compared to France, the details of a Jewish circumcision. But Montaigne's status would cushion him from the sleaziest aspects. Like many visitors he was much taken by Rome's universalism, 'a place where strangers and differences of nationality matter least ... everyone is as if at home' (3).

Rome was expanding fast. The population rose to around 100,000 by the turn of the century. A huge amount of excavation, restoration and new building was going on, reaching a climax in the late 1580s and early 1590s. Palestrina's daily life would intersect with a rich built environment: the Roman remains and Romanesque churches; the austere Castel Sant Angelo; the Gothic Santa Maria Maggiore; the mainly Renaissance San Giovanni Laterano; the brilliant Sistine Chapel decorated by Michelangelo not long before. Elaborate villas and gardens were emerging on the outskirts. The slow rebuilding of the basilica of St Peter's made for a continuing drama, its imposing dome not completed until 1592, while the frontages of some brand new churches were showcasing the forthcoming Baroque in its initial phase of noble simplicity. Palestrina's musical creativity seems likely to have been influenced by this fabulous urban landscape.

A RELIGIOUS CULTURE

Controversies about late 16th 'Counter Reformation' or 'Reform' Catholicism are likely to influence our view of Palestrina and his religion. Critics focus on the autocratic, cruel or persecuting features, others emphasise Catholic anxiety and defensiveness in the face of the Protestant Reformation. Church patronage of the arts may be viewed as an oppressive near-monopoly. Yet another interpretation invokes Counter Reformation creativity, citing reformist movements inside the Church or renewals in devotion, liturgy and religious art.

A view of Palestrina's music as tightly church dictated has been restated by Richard Taruskin. He writes that it was 'arguably a coerced, official style' (even though 'it could be made a very beautiful and moving one') - 'not one that Palestrina or Ruffo {a lesser contemporary} would have adopted spontaneously ...but one imposed by an external force to suit purposes that arguably ran counter to the interests of composers, but that were not negotiable' (4). This view is puzzling. To see Tridentine church authority as tightly monolithic neglects the existence of much confusion and controversy. An ideological or 'modern' concept seems to be at work here, one picturing a composer as culturally autonomous and socially disembodied. To view Palestrina as straight-jacketed, even contrary to his own inclinations, seems a caricature.

As to his exposure to some of the harder edges of late 16th century Catholicism there can be little doubt. He lived under an increasingly centralised theocracy within the papal domain. In common with other Romans, including leading figures inside the church hierarchy, he had to endure the oppressive papacy of Paul 1V (1555-59), a frightening, deeply unpopular man with paranoid tendencies. The reign of Pius V (1565-72), saintly yet narrow, uncultured and erratic, can hardly have been congenial. Other popes, though, would be sympathetic and helpful, notably Gregory X111 (1572-1585). Palestrina would witness the papal-official rejoicing over the Massacre of Huguenots in France in 157O. He would compose effusive musical tributes to the pope relating to the victory over the Turks at Lepanto in 1571. However, church constraints on musical composition were relatively mild in practice, even in theory. He was immune from the highly detailed, sometimes onerous instructions, at least as to iconography, which were typically imposed on painters or architects. The Inquisition and the Index, sometimes harsh towards writers, scientists or philosophers (though less extreme than in Spain) posed no threat to him.

Quite reasonably, there has been some emphasis on Palestrina's pitches for high rewards for jobs and for musical works, his eye for lucrative new markets, his apparently canny management of the skin and fur business. Most of these activities are classifiable as run-of-the-mill family obligation or standard professionalism.

As to the character of Palestrina's religion, his conventionally pious formulae for musical dedications or publications tell us little. Regular attendance at mass we can reasonably assume. Aesthetic influences may well have contributed, including the new or renovated church buildings and the religious art everywhere around including the brilliant frescoes of Ghirlandaio and Pinturicchio and Michelangelo's recently completed masterpieces in the Sistine Chapel. He was clearly well versed in the leading scriptural and liturgical texts. Among works regarded as *de rigueur* for leading Catholics, it would be surprising if he lacked a copy of the authoritative new *Catechism* published in 1566. He would have been aware of the Church Fathers, St Augustine, the great mystics, Thomas a Kempis, St Bernard, St Francis, St Catherine of Siena, and Dante.

Palestrina was a member of the largest lay confraternity of the time, the *Sanctissima Trinita dei Pellegrini*. This focussed on regular prayer, social work and care of pilgrims, enjoying powerful patronage from leading church figures. Palestrina once went for several weeks on a pilgrimage with the confraternity to the Holy House of Loreto, directing music on the way. He composed for the confraternity, though we do not know how far he conformed to its rules for members which included daily prayer, regular communion and charitable outreach (5).

Counter Reformation ideas of 'purification' were relevant to his work. In leading church circles there was a desire to banish pagan models, a sense that idealised forms of nature or human beauty were inadequate to represent the divine. The arts, it was thought, should illuminate theological truths more directly. The cultural and technical advances of the Renaissance were not to be thrown overboard completely but selectively adapted. Luxury was to be demoted, 'holy poverty' celebrated. The Catholic Reformers stressed that religious works of art should be worshipful and serious, avoiding both the 'profane' and the excessively ornate. Giorgio Vasari, praising Michelangelo's eventual turn to piety, was not alone in urging church artists and architects to cultivate personal holiness, an idea with obvious echoes for musicians as well.

There is no firm basis for later idealisations of Palestrina as a kind of musical saint or even as unusually devout. It would be surprising if he lacked a streak of (mostly covert) anti-clericalism common among lay Catholics not least in Rome. He was perfectly capable of standing up assertively for his rights and status. Doubtless too, like many others, he experienced times of tepidity, testing or doubt. However, his persistent exposure to the spirituality and aesthetic of the Catholic Reform, if anything more than to its tougher features: his move towards the priesthood in 1580-81: and not least the sheer persistence of his record as a devoted church musician - all have to be taken seriously.

CHURCH MUSIC FOR HEARTS AND MINDS

A traditional spiritual idealism about music had revered its potential to reflect beauty, goodness and truth, and more specifically to speak of God. For major church figures like Dionysius, Boethius, Augustine, Hildegarde and Aquinas, music on earth was an imperfect reflection of a timeless, perfect music in heaven. They shared with Jewish tradition the idea of a heavenly chorus of angels eternally praising the Most High. Subject to criteria of consonance (for discord was associated with hell and Satan), the idea was that music had or *should* have a special ability to manifest heavenly things, to proclaim God and to symbolise His attributes.

In the late sixteenth century this interpretation was still acknowledged. However, a more 'functional' approach was advancing, a greater focus on the worshipper's state of mind and spirit, which tended to neglect the symbolic aspect. Music's principal role, according to the authorities, should be to foster attitudes of devotion, prayer and loyalty to the Church. It should contribute to the Catholic

Counter Reformation's 'hearts and minds' strategy to attract and mobilise the faithful. An influential senior bishop of the time was typical in insisting that the music of the Mass should 'move our affections to religion and piety'. Giovanni Animuccia, a leading singer and associate of Palestrina, put it more generally. A balance between variety and simplicity: a diverse deployment of voices: economy in 'imitations or inventions' - all were important in the interests of textual messages 'so that their effectiveness, with the aid of the harmony, might penetrate more sweetly the hearts of those who listened'.

The hearts and minds objective was imperiously stipulated by Cardinal (later Saint) Carlo Borromeo, a powerful churchman and a tight disciplinarian in his archdiocese of Milan. Borromeo insisted in an instruction to Vincenzo Ruffo (a more pliable composer than Palestrina), 'that the powerful and sweet sound of the voices should soothe and caress the ears of the listeners in a pious, religious and holy way'. Archbishop Alessandro de Medici (later pope for a short period in 1605) described vocal polyphony as 'a good, useful and holy thing'. Presenting a book of vocal scores to a convent of nuns in his archdiocese of Florence, he wrote,

> 'Knowing that you sing masses and vespers in polyphony, and seeing that for you it is edifying and for others it gives pleasure to hear you, I decided to give you the present book ... As you see, it is music for masses and vespers, which I give to you so that you might praise God in your divine office and at mass, with this new manner of singing. It seems to me that the notes are not so difficult that you would not know how to sing them' (6).

Meantime the exiled English priest Gregory Martin, as usual a fervent enthusiast, would praise the music in the Sistine Chapel, emphasising its liturgical fitness and textual clarity.

> 'The quyer standeth a loft at one side with voyces like so many belles turneable one to an other. No organs bycause the quyer is so ful for al partes. No descant, but such pricke song as every syllable may be heard in thy eares like a Preachers voice'.

Footnotes

(1) Craig Monson, 'The Council of Trent revisited', *Journal of the American Musicological Society,* volume 55, no 1, Spring 2002. This updated and qualified some previous interpretations.

(2) Gregory Martin, *Roma Sancta* (1581), *ed* George B. Parks, Edizioni di Storia e Letteratura, Rome 1969, 48-9, 63-4, 75-8, 86-8, 90, 93-4, 96.

(3) Michel de Montaigne, *The Complete Works, trans* Donald M. Frame, Everyman's Library, 2003, 1149, 1157, 1164, 1167, 1171, 1173.

(4) Richard Taruskin, *The Oxford History of Western Music, Volume 1*, Oxford 2010, 653.

(5) Noel O'Regan, Institutional Patronage in Post-Tridentine Rome: Music at Santissima Trinita dei Pellegrini 1550-1650, Royal Musical Association, London 1995.

(6) K.J.P. Lowe, *Nuns' Chronicles and Convent Culture in Renaissance and Counter Reformation Italy,* Cambridge 2003, 274.

Chapter 3

Love Poetry and Devotional Diversities

Chapter 1 argued for an initial focus on Palestrina's total sound. Highbrow or purist prejudices should not be allowed to discourage a relaxed, free-wheeling sort of listening experience. But as well as being necessary for complete newcomers, the latter is also valuable for the musically literate and even for those already familiar with 16th century music. The total sound seems to be what Palestrina himself had in mind for the large majority of people likely to hear his music, namely church-goers. It is how most people have experienced his music since, whether inside or outside church. It can be rewarding for emotion, mind and spirit, and I will continue to discuss its role as this book develops.

That more structured ways of listening are also important hardly needs stating, however. The composer Aaron Copland writes, 'When you listen to music of Palestrina or Orlando di Lasso, you must listen differently from the way you listen to Schubert or Chopin', since 'polyphonic texture implies a listener who can hear separate strands of melody sung by separate voices, instead of hearing only the sound of all the voices as they happen from moment to moment, vertical fashion'. Copland argues for 'making a mental effort to disentangle the interweaving voices'. This, he suggests, makes listening several times over specially rewarding. 'Repeated hearings keep up your interest better than music of homophonic texture'; 'you can always hear it from a different angle'; there can be 'a greater intellectual participation' (1).

The first essential is to pick up the melodic lead in a work, more often than not a key feature. The usual practice in Palestrina's time was to employ a piece of traditional chant, a popular tune or an existing polyphonic work, the composer's own or someone else's. Often quite simple in form, the melodic lead would be used as a starting point or emblematic opener in a work, then something to be imitated or more likely elaborated as well as bandied about between the voice parts: overall, a structural cell, motif or building block.

The following illustration shows a cross section of Palestrina's melodic leads as entry themes. They occur in 15 of his Mass settings at the start of their *Kyrie eleison* sections.

Note the generally small intervals and the comfortable voice ranges. Also bear in mind a general characteristic of this 16th century music, a rhythmic freedom unconstrained by bar lines (later on bar lines were typically inserted in musical scores because they helped singers to learn a work and keep together in the early stages of singing it together). The non-metricality, showing the influence of previous centuries of free flowing plainchant, is emotionally and spiritually important in Palestrina's music, not least in helping towards a 'floating' quality.

Palestrina followed a generally accepted practice during this period which involved sometimes using other composers' melodic leads, in some cases whole sections of their works. One example of the former practice was the melodic lead he used for his Mass *Nasce la gioja*, a jolly, popular tune which came from a contemporary, Primavera. The important thing was what you did with such material, and Palestrina went on to do wonders with this one in the *Kyrie* and later sections of the *Nasce la gioja* Mass. Although these melodic leads are usually unremarkable in themselves, listeners will find them useful as emblematic starting points in a work or when a new section of text is introduced.

Some of the melodic-rhythmic leads are catchy, jingly, easily hummable, and readers may enjoy trying this out (*Tu est Petrus, Ave Maria a 4*). The *Assumpta est Maria* one has a simple compact curvature. A further category is undulatingly horizontal, resembling decorated or sculpted friezes around buildings or their entablatures. The *Papae Marcelli* lead motif lies at the simple end of this spectrum, whereas others run to ornateness with quaver notes and longer spans, the two-fold syncopation and lilting quality in the *Viri Galilei* motif being particularly attractive. Perhaps most striking is an undulating ascent. Here the upward-moving curve includes lesser curves or inflections and a melismatic element (for example in *Benedicta es*).

It goes without saying that a live performance, where one sees both singers and conductor, provides the most vivid experience of vocal polyphony – not only the melodic leads at the start but also the different mixtures of parts as the voices come and go in what follows.

The first opportunity to pick out a melodic lead occurs during the opening phase of a work since the voice parts typically enter separately one by one (see the *Dilectus meus* example in chapter 1). This can provide just enough time for a listener to get an idea of each part with a better chance of distinguishing them later when things get more complicated. But you have to be fairly quick about it. The parts tend to join in fairly rapidly and a work's opening phase is brief. Palestrina's favourite approach is to sequence the melodic lead downwards, from high to middle to lower parts. Sometimes, though, the process works from bottom to top, or else the initial impetus comes from a middle part or parts, the tenors or altos, who are then joined from above *or* below.

An emphasis on voice part listening needs qualifying in view of Palestrina's use of homophony. His chordal episodes add touches of variety. Chords are able to emphasise a vivid event within the narrative (for example, the words *et subito*, 'and suddenly', or 'the Spirit filled each one' in a Pentecost motet). They may be used to pose a question (as when a group of women asks a friend about her beloved young man in a *Song of Songs* motet). Often they nicely embody a collective statement (like 'we have wrought injustice', or 'let us rejoice'). But as already emphasised, the dominant feature in this music is counterpoint. So Copland is right, that if you are going to enjoy Palestrina's music to the full, an essential is sensitivity to the distinctiveness and interweaving of the voice parts.

FROM SECULAR TO SACRED-EROTIC

Palestrina's network was not exclusively churchy. One important connection – with Cardinal Ippolito 11 d'Este, a member of the princely family of Ferrara - seems to have been largely secular. Ippolito, builder of the superb Villa d'Este and its celebrated gardens just outside Rome, was a highly cultivated, wealthy patron at the worldly end of the post-Tridentine cardinalate, an occasional impresario, a favourite dedicatee for leading artists and poets. Palestrina composed and conducted for Ippolito at various times after 1564 and spent some time directing the music in his well resourced private chapel between 1567 and 1571. This connection would involve exposure not only to aristocratic cultural standards but also to pagan classical models in literature, painting and sculpture.

Palestrina got going with secular music at an early stage. A *First Book of Madrigals*, published in 1555, set texts of love poetry, some by Petrarch, revealing the poet's long, troubled relationship with his mistress Laura. The texts tend to be repetitive, sometimes playful, often exuding pathos. The madrigals are four-part pieces, sometimes featuring at least 50% of homophony and a lot of rhythmic motion. This music is not outstanding as madrigal material and no one appears to claim it as a peak in Palestrina's art, though it is pleasurable to hear the Italian texts when nicely sung. The music is well within the capacity of good amateur singers, though better suited to private than public performance.

A second madrigal collection, published much later in 1586, continues with lyrical love poetry. Sorrow and tears outweigh joy or hopefulness, very much on a Petrarchan note of volatility or transience in love. Palestrina's treatment is such that the expressiveness around such words as *combattendo, lagrime, dolor, pianti, morte* is restrained. The pieces are longer than those published earlier, the counterpoint more pervasive. The style is temperate, the ethos delicate and urbane. There was a growing demand for music of this kind, typically for use in the home, with scope for instruments which could fill in, double up or even substitute where voices were lacking.

A more advanced level emerges in Palestrina's settings from the *Song of Songs*. Here are beautiful Old Testament texts which combine vivid erotic material with long-familiar religious interpretations. Having already set some excerpts for a feast devoted to Mary, by 1584 Palestrina was ready to go public with 29 pieces within his fourth book of motets, a publication that would prove highly popular. In a dedication to Pope Gregory X111 he took the opportunity to express regret, even repentance for the worldly character of these and other earlier works, and he made a point of stressing Christian sacred readings of the *Song of Songs*.

This excited later controversy. A 17th century critic, Luigi Zacconi, would express prim moral disapproval of the erotic material; the leading Palestrina revivalist, Giuseppe Baini, prone to idealise the composer's piety, would conjure up a romanticising tale about some special spiritual rapport with Pope Gregory; while the musicologist Alfred Einstein, evidently keen on a purely secular and erotic reading of the texts, would accuse Palestrina of outright hypocrisy.

In fact, the *Song of Songs* stands out in the Old Testament for its lack of explicit theological content and its vivid love poetry (2). Some previous composers had exploited the sensual aspects of many of the texts with great gusto. However, Palestrina's claim to a religious emphasis had a long history. It reflected an allegorical or metaphorical interpretation, one with a Christian legacy and Jewish antecedents, part influenced also by Platonic or Platonising thought. Here was a culture which tended to view secular phenomena as reflections, signs or symbols of the divine. Hence the love poetry could be associated with the love between God and believers or the Church, or between the soul and Christ. Texts celebrating the beauty and nurturing qualities of the female loved one were linked to the Virgin Mary as arch-helper, consoler and mediator.

Although this sacralising bias would have loomed large for Palestrina, with its 'take' on the human as pale analogue of the divine, he could hardly have been indifferent to the sexual angle. In this respect his dedicatee Pope Gregory was in all likelihood complicit. Gregory, whose natural son Giacomo Buoncompagni, Duke of Sora, was a well-known character in Rome at the time, had been no stranger to sexual experience in his much earlier years (3).

The *Song of Songs* texts which Palestrina set to music in a series of short motets are more erotic, at least in a refined sense, than the earlier madrigal ones. In some of these pieces genders are unclear or seem to switch: in some the lover is clearly male, in rather more it appears to be a woman or women speaking about a man. Parts of the beloved's body are eulogised, being playfully likened to natural objects or artefacts, as for example, eyes to pools of water or doves, neck or thighs to jewels. Breasts feature a lot, often linked with fruits or wine. Kissing or embracing hardly appear; physical union is no more than hinted at. The tone is lyrical, though often intense.

In his dedication to the pope Palestrina applies the term *alacriore*, 'relatively lively'. Expectations of extreme drama are confounded, however, partly by what he does with the text, mainly by what he does *not*. He shuns the advice of an affiliate of Ippolito d'Este's circle, the music theorist Nicola Vicentino, who had argued controversially for the chromatic and for music to shift decisively towards the dramatic and emotional. However, Palestrina's *Song of Songs* music is highly enjoyable both to listen to and to sing. Elegance, symmetry and delicacy abound. The ethos is gently playful. These are not great mountains, but they excel as gardens, meadows, vineyards, orchards.

CELEBRATING THE SENSES

A leading *Song of Songs* motet is number 10, *Vulnerasti cor meum, soror mea sponsa*, 'Thou hast ravished my heart, my sister, my bride'. Here the first phrase sobs out intricate variations on a haunting melodic lead. After a short imitative section the piece moves to dance-like triple time on the words *Quam pulchri sunt mammae tuae*, 'how beautiful are your breasts'. Finally the wines and perfumes of *odor* and *aromata* feature a series of harmonic progressions with much rhythmic interest.

In motet number 19, *Adiuro vos*, a woman calls on some other women, *filiae Jerusalem*, 'daughters of Jerusalem', to help her to find her beloved. Her call grows in urgency, through syncopated repetition, to a sensuous *amore langueo*, 'I languish with love', for good measure uniting all the parts. The women question her: *Qualis est dilectus tuus ex dilecto, O pulcherrima mulierum*, 'What is thy beloved more than another, oh thou, most beautiful of women' ? Her delighted answer, *Dilectus meus candidus et rubicundus, electus ex milibus*, 'My beloved is handsome and radiant, he is one among thousands', comes in free ranging counterpoint.

The opening section of motet number 26, *Duo ubera tua* is shown on the following page. Notice a typical Palestrina feature: the frequency of intervals of one, two or three notes. The beloved's breasts are likened to twin fawns or roes, her nose to a tower of ivory. Her head is likened to Mount Carmel. Later on a phrase about 'the daughter of the multitude' ends with busy downward moving quavers on *multitudinis*. Tenors and basses ascend to high reaches on *sicut turris Libani*, 'like the tower of Lebanon'. The last section offers nicely shared-out rhythmic plays in high registers. Finally, the beloved's hair becomes quasi-monarchical in a phrase *sicut purpura Regis*, 'as in royal purple', ending with each part singing descending quavers on her hair-style, *iuncta canalibus*, 'braided in strands'.

'Pictorialism' in these pieces, where a word or phrase receives quasi-imitative or would-be mimicking musical treatment, requires some comment. For example, in another motet *Nigra sum sed formosa* ('I am black but beautiful') the music is low-registered and seems sultrily dark coloured. In another piece there are curling, melismatic plays on words like *turturis* (turtle doves), *monilia* (jewels), *nardus* (spikenard, fragrant plant). Such quasi-representation tends if anything to be over-emphasised in concert or CD notes, usually

26 - Duo ubera tua

SSATB a cappella

described as 'word painting'. In this respect there is nothing particularly special about Palestrina, and some of his contemporaries do it more graphically. But still, in terms of musical beauty, the *Song of Songs* settings surely rank among the finest of his works.

SPIRITUAL MADRIGALS, OFFERTORIES AND *MAGNIFICATS*

Palestrina's long involvement with religious themes and celebrations raises complex issues. How would his style and structure be affected by the varying contents and purposes of the contrasting texts ? Would the music follow the detailed twists and turns *within* a text ? Could the quality of output be maintained when poured out in such quantities ? How would Palestrina respond to the needs of worshippers, liturgical processes, the subtleties of the relevant doctrines ?

One category of his religious works, the spiritual madrigals, is puzzling. Here are sacred texts but ones neither suited nor intended for normal liturgical use, being more informal than a sacred motet or a Mass setting. Yet his spiritual madrigals are more sophisticated than the unison chordal *laude* or 'praises' which were used by some religious orders or lay confraternities, typically for processions, pilgrim gatherings or oratory devotions. So they tend to fall between stools.

A leading example sets to music a series of Marian lyrics by Petrarch. Each stanza starts with praise of Mary and her role in salvation, then moves to the poet-narrator's troubled entreaties to her for intercession and help. Such to'ing and fro'ing between praise and petition can be effective within a litany, with varying voice combinations and cumulative force building up through ritual repetition. Here Palestrina chooses a homogeneous treatment, and the nobility or éclat evident in other of his Marian works are lacking. However, the music was probably attractive to amateur as well as professional singers in his time either as madrigal material for the home or in devotional contexts apart from regular liturgy. It could still work well enough today in similar contexts or as separately performed short pieces.

One regular church event required a large quantity of musical settings, the offertory within the liturgy of the Mass. Palestrina composed as many as 68 offertories, mostly two or three minute pieces using material from the Old Testament psalms. A large majority of the texts focus on praise and thanksgiving (other psalmic material, especially with more anxious, strident or angry themes, the Church has traditionally chosen to omit). Some call for vigorous singing, others for a calmer, more reflective style. Repeatedly, they express exultation or joy: thus *Jubilate Deo, Benedictus es Domine, Laudate Dominum.*

Palestrina's offertory settings tend to be workmanlike rather than inspired, although some of his admirers would disagree. The sheer quantity of settings required for a less than central part of the Mass could have turned composing into something of a chore, hence some drops in inspiration might be expected. Also there is a wider case for saying that the psalms, with their dense wording and heightened speech rhythms, lend themselves best to unison chant, as practised through the centuries in the daily prayer formats of religious communities, whereas a polyphonic treatment is too elaborate and arguably works less well. All that said, Palestrina's offertory settings have fulfilled a valued liturgical role while some leading commentators and church musicians esteem them highly. Among fine examples are *Improperium, Benedictus sit Deus,* and the ubiquitous Catholic prayer, *Ave Maria.*

For centuries one noble and inspiring text, an Old Testament canticle, has featured in evening services in all the mainstream Christian denominations, the Magnificat. This text has attracted many leading composers from Dufay and Lassus, through Monteverdi, Schutz, Bach and Mozart, on to such as Part and Penderecki, and it plays well to Palestrina's talents.

The *Magnificat* unfolds Mary's response to Elizabeth's prediction of her divine motherhood (Luke 1, 46-55). Mary wonders at God's greatness and the amazing role assigned to her. She sounds a radical note about justice: 'He has put down the mighty from their seats, He has fed the hungry with good things, but the rich he has sent empty away', *esurient humiles et divites dimisit inanes*. The climax comes in the final glorification of the Trinity, *Gloria Patri et Filio et Spiritui Sancto*.

Coming towards the end of Vespers, the principal evening office, fine choral settings would feature in leading churches and basilicas. In the late 16th century these would be encouraged by some Catholic Reform circles, with Jesuits at the forefront, particularly on feast days related to Mary. One can readily picture the lavish scenario on a major feast day during a Palestrina setting. Richly vested priests, altar ablaze with candles, all eyes on the tabernacle containing the consecrated elements, solemn genuflections, clouds of incense.

With a single exception Palestrina's 35 *Magnificats* alternate chant and polyphony. We hear two long traditions of sacred music complementing and enhancing each other - primordial plainchant (shared with some other world religions) and the evolved choral polyphony of Latin Western Europe. Most are four-parters, a good example being the compact Book 1 *Quarti Toni* setting. Here the lithely shaped lead motives of each polyphonic verse become progressively more interesting within a compact format. By contrast, an opulent *Primi Toni* setting stands out as exceptional, with two choirs, continuous polyphony and short bursts of declamatory antiphony, tending to anticipate Monteverdi and the baroque.

Certain features tend to recur. An opening call from the deep, the chanted single word *Magnificat*, exerts a haunting later influence. At its starkest only a few notes are involved, immediately followed by a polyphonic *anima mea Dominum*. When the whole phrase *Magnificat anima mea Dominum* is chanted in other cases it is still the first few notes round the word *Magnificat* that tend to re-echo in later verses.

The phrase *et sanctum nomen eius* gets elongated, as if repeatedly bowing at the name of God. The word *Abraham* often obtrudes almost plonkingly: a sudden touch of the brute human. Vocal shapings of the words *esurientes* and *inanes* bring out their elegant sound and stresses. As for the final polyphonic verses - *Gloria Patri* in some settings, *Sicut erat in principio* in others - the words spin out in riveting climaxes and celebrations (in technical terms, doxologies) of the glory and infinity of the Trinitarian God.

One setting is particularly beautiful: a Book 3 *Tertii Toni* with an unusual line-up of voice parts, CAATTB. Here Palestrina, often at his most resourceful with the middle voices, encourages the alto and tenor resonances. Counterpoint enters on *et exsultavit* with two melodic leads sung simultaneously, one agile and dexterous, the other ultra-simple and slower. The first few notes of the latter go on to echo hauntingly in various ways at the start of the following verses. The final phrase, *Sicut erat in principio,* an exceptionally long one, is particularly fine. With its move to lilting triple time and brief touches of homophony as the parts chase each other contrapuntally, it makes eternity sound excitingly versatile and 'dancey'.

SACRED EVENTS, PERVASIVE MYSTERY

It is important to understand that Palestrina writes his liturgical motets and related works within a long-established format, the central Christian narrative as followed through in the Church's Year. He composes for a belief system which sees God as unchanging, eternal, infinite, mysterious and in a vital sense unknowable. It is a framework which sets formidable tests for a church musician, particularly so for Palestrina who addresses its every nook and cranny and remains in the thick of it for so long.

Each main phase in the Church Year has its own mood and ethos. Advent calls to mind human frailty and suspenseful expectation, a looking-forward to the Saviour's coming. Exultation follows at Christmas and Epiphany, occasions primarily for joy. The forty days of Lent, reflecting on human wrongdoing, call for restraint and penitence. Sorrow accumulates through the intensities of Holy Week, culminating in the starkness of Good Friday, which re-enact the Passion and Crucifixion. Then come Easter, Ascension and Pentecost, signalling victory, Christ's continued presence, the Holy Spirit. Here the consistent keynote is *glory*, a theme featuring further in celebrations of the Apostles, the chief saints, and Mary's life and leading role.

As to whether these changes should bring dramatic mood swings in the music, both liturgical and theological criteria suggest caution. A high degree of constancy is expected in church music through a year. Quite simply, worshippers are likely to be upset by too many changes. The case for continuity also relates to mainstream Christian beliefs. No great sacred happening can be treated in isolation since the relevant doctrines are interdependent. Thus Christmas contains a hint of eventual sorrow: joy at the advent of God is thought to accompany a correlate belief that Christ has still to come, indeed is 'never finished with coming', so that a joyful 'already' is qualified by a wistful or expectant 'not yet'. Again, Christ's sufferings and death on the Cross are not regarded as final but hailed as redemptive, a prelude to His Resurrection and Ascension in glory.

The belief is that while the Church Year celebrates a sequence of transcendental happenings, namely God's actions in history, more fundamental truths are thereby revealed pertaining to God's eternal nature and being. Correspondingly, worship not only addresses sacred events it also invokes the divine essence and abidingness. A challenging implication follows for the music. Alongside the festal/seasonal variations, should this somehow intimate God as eternal, infinite and merciful, and if so how ? Christianity abounds in amazements, notably the Incarnation and Resurrection of Christ, and the overarching belief in God's eternal nature as Trinity, a perfect, infinite reciprocity of love between Three Persons. There has long been a case for thinking that music is well placed to intimate such mind-boggling 'mysteries of faith' symbolically; in some ways more effectively than texts, verbal preaching or visual imagery.

MUSIC FOR ADVENT, CHRISTMAS AND BEYOND

I want to finish this introductory sample with the first of a series of mountain peaks: Palestrina's settings of the narratives and mysteries around Christ's nativity (later phases in the Church Year will follow in the next chapter). Here are some leading texts he worked on. The momentous story justifies considering them together since there is unity as well as variety in the music he weaves around them.

Hodie Christus natus est, *noe, noe,*	*Today Christ is born, noel, noel,*
Hodie salvator apparuit, noe, noe,	*Today the Saviour comes, noel, noel,*
Hodie in terra canunt angeli,	*Today on earth the angels sing,*
Laetantur archangeli, noe, noe,	*The archangels rejoice, noel, noel,*
Hodie, exultant iusti dicentes,	*Today the just exult, saying:*
Gloria in excelsis Deo, noe, noe	*Glory to God in the highest, noel, noel*
O magnum mysterium,	*How amazing a mystery,*
Et admirabile Sacramentum,	*And how marvellous a sacrament,*
Ut animalia viderent Dominum natum,	*that beasts should see the new-born Lord,*
Jacentem in praesepio	*lying in a manger*
Natum vidimus et choros angelorum	*We see the infant and the angelic choir*
omnium, Alleluia	*together praising the Lord, Alleluia*
Quem vidistis, pastores ?	*O shepherds, what did you see ?*
Dicite, annunciate nobis,	*Speak, tell us,*
Quis apparuit ?	*Who has appeared ?*
Natum vidimus,	*We have seen the new-born*
et choros angelorum	*and choirs of angels*
collaudantes Dominum, Alleluia	*together praising the Lord, Alleluia*

Surge illuminare, Jerusalem	*Arise and rejoice, O Jerusalem,*
Quia venit lumen tuum	*for a light has come to you*
Et gloria Domini	*and the glory of the Lord*
Super te orta est.	*has come upon you.*
Quia ecce tenebrae operient terram,	*For behold, darkness shall cover the earth*
Et caligulo populos;	*and mists come over the people;*
Super te autem orietur Dominus,	*But the Lord shall arise upon you,*
Et gloria eius in te videbitur	*and you will see his glory.*

Palestrina's motets on these texts are typically compact, also relatively full-voiced. He deploys six parts in one, two choirs in the others, providing a lot of scope for antiphony. He tacks certain devices onto solemn key words: thus, long note values for *Christe, Gloria, Domini,* and a specially striking, long drawn-out initial '*O*' in *O Magnum Mysterium*. Catchy rhythmic features spring out at the following points: *Noe, noe; collaudantes, dicit, annunciate, et gloria eius*. On *canunt*, 'sing', and *Alleluia*, winding melismas of 'dancey' quavers take centre stage. Typically, Palestrina gets the *tutti* to converge all-out in final sections. He also springs some surprises.

Hodie Christus natus est, a simple proclamation, rings out like a silvery fanfare with cries of *Noe, noe* in short, sharp bursts. It comes close to the rousing, hearty end of the spectrum of popular Christmas carols. The piece achieves impact primarily through strong, simple rhythms, particularly on *Noe, noe*, and through repeated near-antiphonal exchanges between two choirs, with partial biasses towards high or lower voices. The running melismatic passages suggest the singing of angels. The final brief section of *Noe, noe* strikingly moves to lilting, rocking triple time.

The text of *O Magnum Mysterium* packs in exceptional devotional and theological punch. The setting starts with a series of chords expressing breathless wonder at the divine mystery. Then we move through the earthiness of beasts, infant and manger, rising finally to the heavenly choirs. Other composers of the time produce settings of comparable quality to Palestrina's. However, his sensitive handling

Love Poetry and Devotional Diversities   45

of the words is impressive. The phrases spin out to 14 minim beats, equivalent to seven or eight bars. They follow a typical Palestrina curve, slow on the ascent, faster on the descent. The rocking triple time rhythms of *collaudantes Dominum* towards the end are riveting.

Once again small intervals dominate: through 78 bars there are no more than 27 fourths, 14 fifths, and four octaves. The concluding *Alleluias* are superb. Their final gyrations are shown below. Notice a feature which is typical of Palestrina also in his slower music, as in the *Dilectus meus* example in chapter 1: the frequency of off-beat entries, contributing to rhythmic freedom within a steady overall pulse.

The text of *Quem vidisti pastores ?*, sequel to O *Magnum Mysterium*, includes (1) a question-and-answer episode between bystanders and shepherds, (2) a move through time as the amazing news unfolds, and (3) a vertical ascent, as it were, as we progress from human exchanges, through the sight of the divine child, thence to angels and heaven, terminating with *alleluias*. In the dialogue section *Quem vidisti pastores ?* emerges as nicely interrogative, *dicite* ('speak') as imperious, *annunciate nobis* ('tell us') as insistent, even impatient, and *Quis apparuit* ('who has appeared ?') as suspenseful, almost bated breath. The shepherds' reply, *natum vidimus* (broadly translatable as 'we saw the new-born baby') is aptly matter of fact. The final sections reprise the last part of the preceding *O Magnum Mysterium*. On *Et chorus angelorum* the angels seem to take over in a triple time dance, three times over, AATB, then SSAB, then *tutti* on *collaudantes Dominum*, and once again we hear the exultant *alleluias*.

My last example is the eight part *Surge illuminare, Jerusalem*. The text from Isaiah, sensitively followed by Palestrina, moves from excited arousal by divine light, through thoughts of gloom, back to a brighter light of the divine glory. Chordal passages work mostly through antiphony, with the full force of all eight voice parts employed for periodic bursts of drama: *et gloria Domini super te orta est*, ('and the glory of the Lord has come upon you'), and *et Gloria eius in te videbitur* ('and you will see His glory').

The motet gets off to a vibrant, almost startling entry with an imitative sequence of short, excited quaver runs on *surge*. The build-up of intensity on *et gloria eius* is unusually drawn-out, running to 29 bars and leading to a superb conclusion. The quality of this motet is exceptional, offering a glimpse of much fine Palestrina still to come.

Footnotes

(1) Aaron Copland, *What to listen for in Music*, Signet Classic, Penguin Group (U.S.A) Inc, 2002, 85-87.

(2) Jessie Anne Owens, 'Palestrina as Reader, Motets from the Song of Songs', in Dolores Pesce, *ed, Hearing the Motet, Essays in the Motet of the Middle Ages and Renaissance*, Oxford 1977, 307-311. The following section draws extensively on this chapter.

(3) As a law professor in Bologna, 1531-39, Ugo Buoncompagni, the future Gregory X111, 'led a free life and had a natural son, Giacomo': J.N.D. Kelly, the *Oxford Dictionary of Popes*, Oxford 1988, 269. Gregory, a long-tenured and in many ways capable pope as well as a supportive patron of Palestrina, is unfairly discounted by Eamon Duffy in *Saints and Sinners, A History of the Popes*, Yale 1977, 170, as simply 'another man of the world'.

Chapter 4

Sorrow, Suffering, Hope and Glory

Here is the text of a famous Palestrina motet *Super flumina Babylonis,* with its haunting theme of desolation in exile and captivity (psalm 126, verse 1).

Super flumina Babylonis,	By the waters of Babylon,
Illic sedimus et flevimus	We sat down and wept
Dum recordaremur tui, Sion:	When we remembered you, Sion:
In salicibus in medio eius,	On the willow trees in their midst
Suspendimus organa nostra.	We hung up our harps.

The work has a firm tonal continuity, in modern terms A minor. Starting with the bass line, the four parts CATB enter in turn with a plangent melodic lead on *Super flumina Babylonis*. On *illic sedimus et flevimus,* fittingly for a collective statement, the parts converge chordally. Further melodic lines follow on *Dum recordaremur tui, Sion* and *in salicibus in medio eius,* the latter featuring rhythmic repetition. In the final phrase, *suspendimus,* we seem to hear the 'hanging' *via* simple, rhythmically insistent phrases, repeated 14 times in varying forms. Towards the end are some fine suspensions, where a dissonant interval is musically suspended before being resolved, giving a sense of tension, then relief.

Another work on the landscape of desolation is relatively neglected, the motet *Tribulationes civitatum* involving more voice parts (CATTB) and a more intricate text. Here again is a painful communal experience but one leading to an emotional shift and something of a moral progression.

Tribulationes civitatum audivimus	We have heard of the trouble in the city
Quae passae sunt et deficimus.	Shattered and dispersed, we have fled.
Timor et hebetudo mentis cecidit	Fear and dread fell upon us and on our children
Super nos, et super liberos nostros	Lord have mercy
Domine miserere	
Peccavimus cum patribus nostris	With our forefathers we have sinned;
Iniuste egimus, iniquitatem fecimus.	We have wrought injustice, we have done
Domine miserere.	Evil things. Lord have mercy.

To begin with, ascending phrases on *tribulationes* culminate with an accent on the 'o', a sensitive piece of word setting. One melodic lead comes successively from each of the tenor parts followed by the cantus, another from the basses followed by the altos. The melodies gather intensity as they interweave. Later, after an unusual pause, the word *timor*, 'fear' or 'dread', stands out starkly. The final phrase, *Domine miserere*, comes in three waves: first, some largely descending curves, then high register intensifications, then lines slightly falling away.

Part 2 brings a shift in emphasis. *Peccavimus cum patribus nostris* starts with a rather heavy feel, stressing the 'a' in *peccavimus*, as if recalling the primordial sin, and breaking into long melismas on *nostris*. The parts contribute in turn, as if expressing each group's complicity. A more mature conscience emerges with the words *iniuste egimus, iniquitatem fecimus*. This passage expresses collective penitence *via* brief touches of homophony. The final *Domine miserere* broadly echoes its part 1 predecessor with largely falling figures, the context now pointing to a reflectively contrite plea for forgiveness.

These are interesting motets and well recorded, taken from my sample of more than 80, and some others will follow in this chapter. I should warn the reader, though, about a frequent problem with Palestrina's motets. You will have to pick your way. A singer will be faced with a score which she can straightaway get to work on, but if you just want to listen you may well find that the recording you want is part of a mixed assortment. A few collections focus on a particular theme, which may be helpful. More likely, the recording you seek will be included alongside a related larger work, usually a whole Mass setting.

Some of the motets in my selection are intended for normal Sundays or, in church parlance, 'ordinary times'. A few stand out like the celebrated *Sicut Cervus* (on the text 'As the hart desires the water, so my soul longs for Thee, O God'). Among those dedicated to individual saints the motets *Beatus Laurentius, Venit Michael* and *Valde honorandus est* (the last in honour of Saint John the Baptist) do justice to these holy figures. Saint Peter inspires the famous motet *Tu es Petrus* with its catchy rhythms and vivid climax on the words *et tibi dabo claves regni coelorum* ('and I will give you the keys of the kingdom'). Less well known is a more reflective piece on the same theme, *Tu es Pastor ovium*. Both of these embody Counter Reformation Catholicism, vigorously emphasising papal primacy.

SORROW, SUFFERING AND DEATH

When it comes to these themes in the Church Year Palestrina could have hyped up a dramatics of pathos, as some other composers were doing. But although this would have chimed with some current developments in ecclesial Rome as 'a workshop of sacred oratory', he repeatedly avoids exaggeration and manneristic rhetorical gesture. The meaning of a text is conveyed more subtly by means of imaginative vocal scoring or gentle emphasis. Emotion is never absent but always in dignified fashion and qualified by a sense of reflectiveness (1).

Notable examples include *Heu mihi, Domine,* ('Here, it is me, Lord'), a CATB piece within the capacity of an average choir, which achieves clarity and pungency in delivering its psalm text with due sadness but without self-pity. I strongly commend it. The better known *O Bone Jesu, exaudi me* ('Good Jesus, hear me') is more elaborate with six parts CCATTB. These texts speak of death. They acknowledge sinfulness and a need for forgiveness. Key words are treated expressively but with economy and restraint, notably *mortis* (death) and *miser (*wretch, poor creature). There are touches of trust and hope. Thus after much sombre material *O Bone Jesu* ends with a phase of rejoicing with angels *in saecula saeculorum,* while another penitential motet *Peccantem me quotidie* concludes with a gentler healing phrase on *et salva me.* In both cases the rounding-out arrives through a liquefying, relatively relaxing counterpoint.

As the Church Year unwinds through the six weeks of Lent sacrifice and repentance are the dominant themes. Ash Wednesday forms the sombre starting-point with its symbolic use of dust and ashes as reminders of mortality. Towards the end of Lent the intensities of Holy Week include Palm Sunday, which re-enacts Christ's entry into Jerusalem with processions of people holding palms, and Maundy Thursday, the solemn celebration of the Last Supper. On Good Friday long tracts of scripture are chanted, again with processions, this time kneeling and kissing the cross. Statues are covered, vestments and curtains coloured purple or black. There is an exceptional pile-up of liturgical texts: Old Testament excerpts interpreted as prophesying or symbolising Christ's sacrifice, relevant poetry and hymnody, the Gospel narratives of the Passion.

During Holy Week large quantities of music have to deliver long texts and enhance the ceremonies, including the crowd movements. In part, Palestrina's response is ultra-traditional, restating an idiom with primordial roots in virtually all religious traditions, that

Sorrow, Suffering, Hope and Glory 53

of repetitive lament. He sets a text for Good Friday, *Popule Meus*, commonly known as 'the reproaches', in the verse/refrain format we encountered in the *Magnificat* (last chapter). The refrain makes its point partly in Greek: *Agios O Theos, Agios ischyros, Agios athanatos, eleison imas*, 'Holy God, Holy and Strong, Holy and Immortal, have mercy on us'. Here Palestrina's music is fine for its context, though some of his near-contemporaries responded as beautifully and with a more overt melancholy, notably Tomas Luis de Vitoria.

Ritual-repetitive lament winds out for much longer in Palestrina's *Lamentations*. These are settings of a lengthy Old Testament text attributed to Jeremiah (*Tribulationes civitatum* was an extract, see above). They mingle pure lament with reproaches to the Lord and appeals to His compassion. In one setting we hear long sequences of chords which tend to unblock and liquefy, a typical Palestrina gambit. We are wracked by periodic wailing melismas unexpectedly using Hebrew words. We are almost mesmerised by a repeated refrain, 'Jerusalem, return to the Lord thy God'. It was customary to divide singing of the *Lamentations* between Maundy Thursday, Good Friday and Holy Saturday. Listening all through to a whole recording of the *Lamentations* is for the intrepid, though rewarding for a student or for focussed meditation.

Many people believe that Palestrina's best work for Holy Week is his *Stabat Mater*. The text, a neat-rhyming, not particularly distinguished medieval Latin poem by Jacopone da Todi, circles round Mary's heart-rending experience through her Son's Passion and Crucifixion. Palestrina's rendering is unusually long for a motet (typically lasting nine or 10 minutes). Also unusually for him, it features two choirs CATB/CATB. Although mistakenly supposed to be typical of his music during the romantic revival in the 19th century, the *Stabat Mater* is undeniably one of his finest works. Emotion is never overdone, tragedy emerges cumulatively and inexorably, grief is somehow conveyed as blessed.

Through most of the work the two choirs alternate more or less antiphonally to solemn declamatory effect. The start is deceptively simple: a series of chords featuring a nice harmonic progression: in modern terms A major/G major/F major/C major/F major/G minor/A major. At the end of choir 1's opening statement a suspended fourth in the tenor line is the first in a series of suspensions a lot more frequent than is usual in Palestrina. Their tensions and releases produce subtly wracking climaxes. There are frequent pauses (another unusual feature), occasional changes of rhythm or time signature, some voice part thinnings, and brief spasms when the two choirs converge in full force, as on the phrases *O quam tristis, Sancta Mater istud agas, Fac ut portem Christi mortem*. Even in this largely chordal work, though, counterpoint has the last word as the text climaxes on *Paradisi Gloria*, a beautiful glimpse of heaven.

Alongside the *Stabat Mater* is a relatively neglected work, one that surely ranks as outstanding whether as musical construct, text enhancement or enactment of liturgical drama, while also conveying the mystery. Here is the text of the *Improperium* (based on Psalm 68, 21-22) for the offertory on Palm Sunday.

Improperium expectavit cor meum	My heart has expected reproach
Et miserium	And misery
Et sustinui qui simul meum	And I looked for one that would
Contristaretur et non fuit	Grieve with me and there was none
Consolatem me quesivi et non	I sought for one to comfort me
Inveni et dederunt in	And I found none, and they gave me
Essam meam fel et in siti mea	Gall for my food, and in my thirst
Potaverunt me aceto.	They gave me vinegar to drink.

The interest here lies mainly in word setting, vocal configurations and onward propulsion. The parts move through similar orbits with convex, concave or undulating semi-horizontal melodic lines, their staggered pathways broadly parallel in shape. Sighing prolongations gather round *et miseriam*. The bad news in *et non fuit* ('and there was none') comes *via* short, quick-echoing phrases, markedly so when we reach *et non inveni* ('and I found none'), in the latter case with some notes expressively flattened. The word *aceto* (vinegar) suffers several passing dissonances. There is a sense of something that *has* to happen. The vocal scoring changes on the final phrase *et in siti mea potaverunt me aceto*. Downward moving phrases seem to signal acceptance despite the pain.

If affliction is lightened with a glimpse of transfiguration, if suffering has an ability to point eventually to truth, goodness and beauty, one hears how this would be.

STABILITY, BALANCE AND FLUIDITY

We have now sampled a sufficient range of Palestrina's works - through varying texts, occasions and purposes - to venture a first attempt at an overall perspective.

As we listen we tend to experience certain feelings or physical effects. In particular, thoughts may come to mind of visual objects. Although we may be reluctant to admit such experiences, perhaps fearing highbrow disapproval, they can be enriching. In fact, visual metaphors have a lively background in the history of reception of music, one too little recognised.

A classic example comes from a pre-1945 music scholar, Donald Tovey. Writing about the cadenza of Mozart's quintet in E flat, Tovey suggests that this 'feels like finding one's way through an enormous park, where avenue, glade and copse bewilder us in their endless succession, and vistas open suddenly when we think the prospect is closing in'. In a further instance he experiences in Mozart's Adagio in E major an overall effect 'much as the lights and shadows on a building vary with the position of the sun'. Many other examples of visual metaphor can be found. They have been ascribed, sometimes by composers to their own work, more often by commentators, for example to the music of Lassus, Wagner, Strauss, Debussy, Messaien (2).

In the case of Palestrina the musicologist Knud Jeppesen writes of 'steady, fluid movement in which the rhythm of one voice fits into the others', and of features resulting in 'a uniform, steadily flowing stream' . I would add that the curves move and overlap in different formations, somewhat like the waves of the sea. Indeed, music like Palestrina's can make one think of a yacht sailing forward on a calm sea towards a far distant, perhaps mysterious destination. As in Tovey's image the experience may be partly physical so that, in addition to picturing the scene, we seem to feel the motion of the boat. Alongside the visual image a vicarious bodily feeling can develop, one of calmly floating or moving with the music.

Franz Liszt, a romanticising enthusiast, likened some of Palestrina's music to 'a sonorous incense which carries prayer aloft on its clouds of gold and azure'. For the church musicologist Joseph Samson Palestrina's counterpoint evoked 'needlework' or 'lace'. The term 'kaleidoscopic' has been applied to his mercurial redeployments of voice parts. After hearing music by Palestrina and Lassus in Rome in 1885, Claude Debussy, who was fascinated by wider ideas of relationships between music and the visual arts, wrote of 'winding melodic lines that recall illuminated manuscripts and ancient missals', later adding, perhaps more fittingly, 'melodic arabesques'. In a simpler way affinities can be drawn with the shapes of Palestrina's surroundings: the landscape around *citta* Palestrina, Rome's seven historic hills, the rolling landscapes he would have walked through in Tuscany or Umbria.

In general, religious painting in late 16th century Italy was going through a downturn in quality, but some of its typical devices are relevant. Some painters were applying *cangiantismo* (changeable colour) to the draperies of major figures, its name derived from *seta cangiante (*shot silk). Depending on their angle of vision, viewers would see a luminous irridescence or different colours. Another device was *sfumato*, 'smokiness', previously used to great effect by Leonardo da Vinci and Correggio, 'a soft evanescence in which the outlines and the volumes of the forms seem to vanish in almost imperceptible shifts from dark …..like the flickering of the flame on a candle'. It is possible to find similar effects in the shimmering qualities of Palestrina's polyphony and its mercurial changes of texture.

Moving from visual metaphor to intrinsic structure and style we can get closer to an overall perspective with thoughts of a combination of stability, balance and fluidity.

First, **stability** in Palestrina is ensured by a regular pulse and gentle beat or *tactus* (qualified by elements of rhythmic freedom, see below). Vocal acrobatics are absent. Small intervals, a rarity of fourths or fifths and still more of octaves or still bigger leaps, contribute to an underlying steadiness. The influence of plainchant is evident in these gradual largely stepwise movements. In a wider sense there is much in Palestrina's reiterative patterns to make us think of primitive incantation or recursive prayer. We can readily hear the cyclical, the mantra, the wheel.

Second, **balance and equilibrium** come about partly through respect for normal vocal ranges and the optimal singing zones for cantus, alto, tenor, bass, a refusal to force the voices towards extremes. Balancing effects also arise from (a) alternating, equalising uses of the different voice parts, (b) a frequency of melodic curves featuring slow ascents complemented by faster descents, and (c) moves between melodically structured and relatively elastic forms of counterpoint within a single work.

Third, it should be clear by now that within these parameters many features combine to create much **fluidity and suppleness**. One is a rhythmic elasticity of melodic lines, often cutting across bar lines, as exemplified by the leads in Palestrina's *Kyrie* sections (chapter 1) and the associated frequency of off-beat entries, as in *Dilectus meus* (chapter 1) and O *Magnum Mysterium* (chapter 3). Suppleness also results from overlapping entries, tendencies for chords to unblock and liquefy, and the frequency of redeployment of voice parts.

In the case of voice part redeployment I looked at wider samples. The following table shows the redeployment frequencies in 15 of Palestrina's Masses in their *Sanctus* and *Agnus Dei 1* sections and in the whole of these settings. The columns show rapid rates of change as a ratio to total bar numbers. Half the redeployments occur on average at rates roughly between 2½ and 3½ bars (the lower and upper quartiles). Wider random checks across my core sample suggested that such frequencies are typical.

	Redeployment rates in 15 Mass settings		
	(1) *Sanctus*	(2) *Agnus Dei 1*	(3) Whole settings
Lowest	6.37	7.60	12.50
Lower quartile			3.63
Median	3.00	2.91	3.00
Upper quartile			2.50
Highest	2.13	2.05	1.61

All of this and more adds up to a style very different from later phases of Western choral music, Baroque, neo-classical or romantic. There is a marked contrast with styles which disclose a large-scale purposive design where everything seems to develop according to a virtuosic master plan. There are few, if any of the discrete panel-like reprises, the terraced formations, the precisely rounding-out *da capos or ritornelli* of formal Baroque. There is a contrast, too, with musics of metamorphosis where startlingly new formations continually appear. Perhaps most striking is the difference from dramatic contrasts of register, tempo, texture or dynamics, processes linked with the mainstream tonal system which so often embodies and generates extreme emotional swings.

Overt grand architecture, internal metamorphosis, markedly conflicting tonal forces, then, all of these are foreign to Palestrina. So of course are situations where the vocal forces are folded into larger structures involving instruments and solo singers. Rather, the voice parts speak directly to us in their distinctive, equal and consonant ways.

FEASTS OF DIVINE GLORY

Returning to the Church Year, a momentous shift in the Christian narrative comes at Easter. Palestrina addresses the cusp of this turning-point in an eloquent motet, *Ardens est cor meum* (CCATB), where we reach the hours following Christ's death and burial. Mary Magdalen has been weeping at the empty sepulchre and the text has her saying: *Ardens est cor meum, desidero videre Dominum meum; Quaero, et non inveni ubi posuerunt eum - Alleluia*; 'My heart is full of desire, I so long to see my Lord, I seek and cannot find him, Alleluia'.

The brevity of the text allows a music of exalted melancholy to fan out hauntingly. Melodic material develops for the most part unobtrusively within the texture. On the word *quaero* ('I seek') tortuous, troubled sequences of melismatic quavers spin out across the parts. In a long final section of winding *alleluias* a minor-sounding treatment consistent with the rest of the work seems strange for a word commonly identified with jubilation. However this may sound to modern ears, these *alleluias* can be interpreted either as celebrating the departed Lord or anticipating His return. The beauty of this motet does ample justice to Mary Magdalen's and the other apostles' confusion and desolation, the more poignant just before the situation is transformed.

Another Resurrection piece is an eight part, two choir setting of a famous 22 line hymn for Easter Sunday, *Victimae paschali laudes*. Here Christ is affirmed as redeemer and conqueror of death. Mary, questioned by the apostles, testifies to seeing Him, and the risen Christ is acclaimed and worshipped. At a suitable tempo this work packs a huge amount of diversity into a roughly four-minute performance span. A two choir variable antiphony: a final *tutti* convergence: subtle part differentiations within each choir: a largely prevailing homophony (splendid in triple time on *surrexit Christus spes me*, 'Christ my hope is risen'): and fine contrapuntal episodes on the words *reconciliavit, dic nobis Maria* and *regnat vivus* – all add to the interest. For an attentive listener this work may be useful as an exercise in voice part identification.

A small, intimate piece addresses the touching human episode of doubting Thomas (John 20, 24-29). Palestrina gives Jesus's words a gentle, steady insistence through the counterpoint: *Quia vidisti me, Thoma, credidisti, Beati qui non viderunt êt crediderunt*, 'Because you have seen me, Thomas, you have believed. Blessed are those not seeing who will still believe'. Fairly precise imitations of a haunting melodic lead dominate bars 1-23. Quaver runs, some of them octave ascents, emphasise the strategic words *credidisti* and *crediderunt*. Harmonising E flats seem to confer a blessing on the 'future believers'.

After the Easter celebrations the Church's Year moves to further mountain peaks now signalling victory and glory, along with wonder and mystery as before. 'Glory' stands for divine attributes of splendour, majesty, marvellousness. It brings into play the aesthetic of the Godhead conceived as supremely beautiful. Theologically, it should be noted, the idea of 'glory' implies far more than a human praise of God ('giving' Him, as it were, praise or glory), rather, it is a matter of proclaiming the glory that is His alone. Human emotion persists, but it is the transcendental side of the human-divine relationship that comes to the fore.

Palestrina comes to this scene with great assets. We know he can convey a strong sense of 'glory', as in *Surge Illuminare* (chapter 3). His largely white note diatonic music avoids a problem inherent in conventional major/minor tonality: a fixation on 'happiness' *versus* 'sadness', a polarisation of musical ideas around 'tension and release'. Whatever advantages major/minor tonality may have for

Christian themes of joy, suffering and reconciliation, these peter out when it comes to the subtler reaches of wonder, glory, mystery. Here pre- (or post-) tonal music can do a lot better for our 21st century ears (as some contemporary composers have shown).

Once again Palestrina could have upped the ante. Some of his contemporaries in Venice were composing grandiosely for larger forces and opulent theatrical effects, also with an eye to the Republic's civic pride and public relations. Before long Baroque composers would exploit the 'big bang' resources of larger choirs *plus* instruments *plus* solo singers. However, even Palestrina's longer works for the summit feasts of glory maintain a certain intimacy and avoid a sense, one might say, of 'taking over' from God. His works in honour of the Resurrection, the Ascension and Pentecost are vivid and dramatic but not overpowering or triumphalist in style.

The motet *Viri Galilei* (CCATTB) celebrates the Ascension. It belongs to Palestrina's early middle period, being published in his *First Book of Motets* in 1569, and it leads to one of his finest Mass settings (chapters 9 and 10). The men of Galilee who have seen Christ ascend are told that He will return (*Acts*, 1, 11). His ascent is related to psalm texts about God 'going up with a merry noise', a trumpet sound, with the Lord preparing a place for Him. This work's sensitive text handling emerges in striking contrasts of vocal scoring. Highlights include musical haloes round the words *Hic Jesus*, 'This same Jesus' (*tutti* singing, augmented note values, melismas). Also notable are exuberant ascents on *ascendit Deus in jubilatione,* fanfare arpeggios on *in voce tubae* ('to the sound of the trumpet'), and cascades of descending figures in a riveting series of *Alleluias*.

An outstanding six-part motet *Dum complerentur* (SSATTB) celebrates Pentecost, telling of the meeting of the Apostles when the Holy Spirit came upon them. Like the *Viri Galilei* motet just mentioned, this is an early middle work, published in 1569, which forms the basis of a later Mass setting (chapters 9 and 10).

62 Palestrina For All

Sorrow, Suffering, Hope and Glory 63

Dum complerentur presents a microcosm of polyphonic formats. Starting with declamatory antiphony, it includes brief chordal passages, vigorous rhythms, two sets of imitations in part 2, and much elastic, free flowing counterpoint. A musical enactment, some have suggested, of 'the Spirit blowing where it listeth'. The extracts above show (1) abrupt chordal syncopations on *et subito* ('and suddenly'), (2) excited babble around *factus est sonus de coelo* ('there came a voice from heaven'), (3) the start of long chains of sinuous, fast moving *alleluias*, and (4) criss-crossing rhythms on *tamquam spiritus vehementis,* continuing through to (5) appropriately *tutti* singing on *et replevit totam domum* ('and the rushing spirit filled the whole house').

Several stylistic features stand out in these extracts, all of them typical in Palestrina's music, including in his less excited works: the sheer variety of voice part mixtures, the frequent voice part redeployments, the many off-beat entries. All of these contribute to the fluidity and suppleness commented on earlier in this chapter, complementing the steadfastness provided by an underlying steady pulse and other features. A look at the scores reinforces the idea of a fluidity running towards outright fragmentation. One is tempted to think of a labyrinth or a jigsaw puzzle where the pieces have got disconnected. Put this together with the listening experience where what seems to matter most, to the contrary, is a sweeping sense of continuous onward flow.

We come finally to two motets devoted to Mary. For the feast day which celebrates the Catholic belief in Mary's body-and-soul Assumption into heaven Palestrina's showpiece is an exultant motet *Assumpta est Maria* SSATTB. Here prominence is given to the higher voice parts (sung in his time by boy trebles, adult male counter tenors, altos or *sopranisti),* a format which will continue in the related Mass setting *Assumpta est Maria.* The high pitches may induce thoughts of a celestial choir *via* a vertical metaphor for heaven. But this departs from Palestrina's general adherence to vocal balance. For Mary's feminity to be expressed through high pitched voices would be crudely literalistic. Also it would risk tedium and banality if repeated in the large number of his works framed round Marian texts or dedications. For Palestrina, rather, it seems that all voices need to be fully employed in Mary's honour.

We find this also in a simpler, relatively neglected motet scored for CATB, within the capacity of a competent church choir, a rendering of the standard prayer *Ave Maria*. Following a long established custom which added tropes to the biblically derived text, here a brief example expresses the hope of eventually coming to see Mary in heaven. Each main clause starts with an ultra-simple fragment of long familiar plainchant. Brief chordal passages occasionally unite two or three parts, expanding to all four on the phrases *ora pro nobis* and *ut cum electis te videamus*. This motet re-presents the cherished text and melodic lines with an overall symmetry, a reflective calm and a gently lilting flow.

Footnotes

(1) It is sometimes suggested that Palestrina's music is 'impersonal' or (in a sense sometimes characterised as liturgically apt) 'unemotional'. But a denial of the role of emotion is hard to sustain. Music, including Palestrina's, tends to express and speak to a wide spectrum of human faculties, emotional as well as physical, intellectual, imaginative, religious, and these hardly fall into discrete categories.

(2) Debussy and Messaien draw links between their own music and colours or paintings. A long line of composers, notably Lassus, Byrd, Haydn, Mozart, Wagner, Liszt, Debussy, Strauss, Stravinsky, Boulez, and American composers in general, have had their music related to visual images by music historians or commentators.

Chapter 5

A Music of Amity & Ideal Community

In the whole context of music history in the West 16th century choral music stands out as a distinctive interregnum. Pure vocalism flourished, with human voices typically singing in un-mediated, transparent formats. Instrumentalism was relatively marginal or under-developed. A three-fold patterning in the choral music was important and will play a central part in my argument. First, each voice part tended to be differentiated; second, the parts were broadly equal in importance; and third, their inter-relationships featured high levels of consonance and cordial mutuality. This blend would soon be superseded. However, it was - and still is – of great symbolic importance. I am going to argue that it has a continuing ability to intimate good interpersonal and social relationships, indeed ideal ones. And although Palestrina is not the only Renaissance composer to exhibit this symbolic potential, he does so with particular consistency, coherence and breadth of outreach.

EXPERIENCING MUSIC AS SYMBOLIC

To begin with, what is meant by the proposition that music can be experienced as 'symbolic' ? How does symbol in music compare with other forms of experience of music as already discussed, specifically quasi-representation or 'pictorialism', and visual metaphor ?

Consider some episodes already cited in this book. When Palestrina scores for high vocal registers on the words 'tower of Lebanon' in the *Song of Songs*, or for wavering melismas on the words *suspendimus* or *quaero*, he is engaging in quasi-representation or 'pictorialism'. Similarly with his passing dissonances on *aceto* (vinegar) in the *Improperium,* his arpeggios on the words *in voce tubae,* or his sudden syncopation on *subito* in the motet *Dum complerentur.* In such cases the music seeks to mimic or enact the text in direct fashion, something we can all recognise easily which is often highlighted in notes for concerts or recordings. Bach's Passion music offers striking examples. When Bach has the furious crowd yelling for Christ to be crucified or when he gets Christ's repentant apostle Peter weeping through the music with wracking chromatic melismas, here are further cases of quasi-representation, what is often called 'text' or 'word painting'.

Interpreting music metaphorically differs from this. Here one associates a piece of music with a material object. Extra enjoyment can be found in thinking about something completely different from the music, often in random fashion, with part of the savour coming from the extremity of the difference, the 'foreignness'. In the last chapter I mentioned visual metaphors experienced while under the spell of Mozart or other composers. I referred to a wide variety of such metaphors which listeners to Palestrina or exponents of his music have instanced over time: flowing streams, yachts, kaleidoscopes, *campagna* landscapes, 'lace', 'incense', 'arabesques'.

Experiencing music as 'symbolic' is more subtle and far reaching than either a reality-mimicking 'pictorialism' or an experience of 'listening as seeing'. It means that certain sorts of music can be taken as representing or connoting big ideas or abstract entities which are emotionally, conceptually or spiritually important for us. Some large phenomenon, experience or belief exists somewhere in our minds waiting, as it were, for an intimation, reflection or reminder. Neither rational discussion nor visual metaphor answers to this need, one that can often be better fulfilled by music. For example, music of certain kinds can get us thinking about major social phenomena: our country and its history, historic cultures, social systems, revolutions, anarchy, wars or dictatorships. It may carry intimations of flux or stability, change or continuity, high social ideals and aspirations, the virtues of moderation, courage or compassion. It may induce thoughts about transcendence, infinity, eternity, the deity.

To symbolise in such ways may be the composer's explicit objective, but often it seems *not* or evidence of such an intention is lacking. More often it is listeners or later generations that discover a meaningful symbol in the music. Apprehension of a symbol is contingent and subjective or *inter*-subjective. A listener may avoid symbolism altogether, happy to enjoy the music in other ways. Tendencies to read symbolic meanings into music can vary significantly over time. That modern listeners find pathos or melancholy symbolised by traditional forms of 'white note' modal folk music, for example, does not mean that earlier generations felt the same.

Musical symbolisation, whether intended or imputed, can be indirect. In some of his pieces on Old Testament texts William Byrd comments on the sufferings of the ancient Israelites but in a way also relatable to his persecuted fellow Catholics in Protestant England. J.S. Bach's church cantata *Ein Feste Burg* is thought to symbolise Lutheran integrity and steadfastness, its noble harmony standing out against a nasty dissonance present in the same work (by implication pagan or papist). The highest philosophy or theology can be 'heard through' or 'read into' the tiniest of musical figures. A *da capo* aria in Bach's St John Passion has been associated with Christ's Resurrection and expected return. The single double octave in C minor at the start of Haydn's *Creation* is taken to hint at 'the imminent fall from Grace' or, in a less devout reading, to symbolise 'infinite, empty space'.

Further examples are not hard to find. One Shostakovitch symphony has been associated with 'some luminous, angelic sphere', another one with 'industrial might'. 19[Th] century romantic works, notably Beethoven's, are commonly associated with intense human experiences of passion, frustration, *sturm und drang*. As for changes between major and minor keys, a pervasive feature in tonal music over the last few centuries, it has long been commonplace to identify these with swings in human experience between war and peace, conflict and resolution, suffering and contentment.

MUSIC AS SYMBOL OF GOOD COMMUNITY ?

The idea that certain kinds of music have the ability to symbolise good, highly sought-after or ideal social relationships is hardly new. Plato, an arch-proponent of this perspective, claimed that harmony, in the sense of right proportion between pitches, created 'agreement of voices' and 'mutual accord' between disparate elements. He believed that music, as well as healing conflicts within the self, could improve civic and social behaviour. Plato also held that musical harmony reflects a mathematically conceived, divinely created, perfect order of the universe, and here many later thinkers would follow his lead. The poet Dryden would distil the idea: 'From harmony, from heavenly harmony, The universal frame began'.

A drawback in Plato's theory, even apart from its outdated cosmology, is that 'harmony' is not an absolute phenomenon. Concepts of 'harmony' in music altered as between the classical Greeks, the Middle Ages and post-16th century Europe, while conventional ideas of what is 'harmonious' could still change. Different cultures and parts of the globe have different ideas on the subject. Moreover, Plato's idea seems in retrospect over ambitious. Can hearing harmonious music really be morally beneficial, helping to create more virtuous people or better citizens ?

What seems more likely is that certain kinds of music can hauntingly reflect our yearnings for such relationships. In the tonal system, Western music's standard diet for centuries, a core feature is an experience of peace or reconciliation attained through struggle so that tension and conflict are essential preconditions for unity or resolution. Often fraternity or love emerge fleetingly or elusively, half-hidden by adverse tonal forces or tantalisingly beyond reach. It is also possible, of course, for a music of extreme anger or despair to sound like a systematic loss, denial or negation of good relationships.

Supposing we are asked to define a 'good' or 'ideal' community. We are likely to rule out situations of coercion, extreme inequality, social discord or selfishness. Most of us would probably say that the members of a 'good' or 'ideal' community would be able freely to express their distinctive talents and identities, to be treated fairly equally, and to be reasonably united and friendly towards each other. In socio-political terms this would translate very broadly into 'liberty, equality and fraternity', or in a neighbouring political formula, 'diversity, fairness and solidarity'. That these values are extraordinarily difficult to combine in practice is crashingly obvious, of course. That they persist in our minds as hopes, aspirations or ideals, however, is no less clear. At stake are concepts of a 'good society', 'worlds we have lost', Utopias or Erewhons, a heaven disbelieved in but still wistfully dreamt of, ethical ideals for political action, social struggle or religiously motivated effort.

Some writers have credited instrumental chamber music with symbolising forms of civilised or courteous interchange. We find references to a musical 'argument', 'dialogue' or 'discussion', a 'rational interchange of thought', a 'philosophical discourse'. The terminology can be nicely transitive, as when the different instruments are described as 'commenting on each other', 'answering each other', 'persuading' or 'learning from each other' (1). With the pure vocality of Renaissance choral music these sorts of interaction emerge as specifically human. It is people in small, recognisable choral groups who are dialoguing, learning from each other, communing with each other.

By the late 16th century choral polyphony had evolved towards a distinctive synthesis. Pure unaccompanied choralism continued to be central. At the same time the hierarchies within previous choral music had largely disappeared. The privileged role of a lead part, the *cantus fermus* or *tenor*, had receded. Instead, an equitable balance between the voice parts had emerged, and the distinctiveness of each one was more fully exploited. Counterpoint was still the dominant structure. Chordalism, involving subordination to the collective, was the exception. Not least important, techniques of ensuring an overarching consonance had reached a fine point of development.

Soon, of course, this combination would recede. Pure choralism would lose its primacy. Through the successive phases of Baroque, classical and 19th century music it was instrumentation that would bound forward in diversity and importance. In opera, cantata or oratorio the chorus would have to take its place alongside solo singers, instruments and orchestra, and the same would broadly apply to church music by such as Monteverdi, Bach, Haydn, Mozart etc. Often the choir would stay silent through instrumental sections or episodes sung by virtuoso singers who were often celebrities and a principal draw for the audience. Chordal music was more prominent, involving domination by the highest voice part, 'the tune at the top', and a secondary role for the other parts. The tonal system, involving frequent dissonance and clear cut contrasts between major and minor keys, would take over.

These developments have been so dominant that the contribution of the 16th century interregnum is easily overlooked. Its distinctive combination of pure choralism with differentiation, equality and consonance is neglected. It is this mixture, however, which Palestrina excels at and carries to particularly intense and far reaching levels.

DIVERSITY, EQUALITY AND CONSONANCE

I have already emphasised how Palestrina's melodic-rhythmic lines are differentiated. This applies even when a melodic lead is followed by strict imitation. Here the theme gets precisely duplicated by another part or parts, but what we hear is the original at a different pitch and with a different voice timbre. It is more usual to find variation. There the first few notes of a melodic lead, its 'head', may exactly replicate the parent, but the later notes or 'tails' will differ from it, often radically so, with note values, intervals and rhythm developing in diverse ways. Finally, there may be looser-limbed statements, so far characterised as free range or elastic counterpoint, which lack the melodic-rhythmic patterning present in both imitation and variation.

First, Palestrina's melodic-rhythmic lines lie within the normal, comfortable ranges of the respective voice parts CATB. It is simplistic to think of such lines as 'independent', as sometimes suggested, given the demands of consonance. More helpful to think in terms of *a singularity or individuality of lines,* combined with *interdependence.*

Second, relationships of *equality* between the parts: I decided to test Palestrina's practice in more detail. I found that his Mass settings often have the trebles, altos and tenors singing between 75% and 85% of the time, with the basses typically at around 65% - 70 %. However, the basses often play a foundational harmonic role. They participate fully in key phrases of text and their sonority adds value, as does an ability to convey solemnity and weight.

At the same time practices of inter-part sharing, alternation or complementarity make for *qualitative* equality. Each part contributes at its own pitch to key textual, melodic or rhythmic statements. Roles of 'leader' or 'follower' are short-lived and tend to alternate. The practice of one part (tenor or treble) acting as *cantus firmus* or *primus inter pares,* as referred to above, occurs only in some of Palestrina's earlier works. Through most of his counterpoint no single part sings on its own for more than a few minim beats, usually much less, typically only part of a melodic lead's first entry. Interesting features are widely parcelled out: for example, different types of variation of a given theme: quaver runs; extra-long notes; intervals of more than a fifth (including the very occasional mid-phrase octave); subtly important sharp or flat note accidentals or passing dissonances. Although it can hardly be a matter of precisely equal chances for all of these things through every work, their allocation is widely spread, and it is usual for important statements in a text to be equally distributed between the parts.

Third, in Palestrina consonance (in the culturally relative sense) reigns virtually supreme. His resistance to the dissonances advocated by some music theorists of the time seems almost visceral. He avoids the extreme ones practised by his contemporary Gesualdo. For such devices seriously to invade church music would have been frowned on by the authorities, but whatever the reasons Palestrina composes as if any serious engagement with dissonance would be deeply distasteful, even perverse. He adheres to careful consonance almost as if his life depends on it.

Regarding the detail of consonance, Palestrina favours major triads especially for final chords. He avoids blatant note-on-note dissonances (in ancient folklore seen as marks of the devil). These could hardly be eliminated completely when aiming for the simultaneous melodic lines to be distinctive, attractive and reasonably smooth. For example, a sustained and melodically important note G in one voice can easily clash with other parts where fluidity and melodic coherence suggest a move to A or F. But Palestrina addresses the problem with such ingenuity that the dissonances are reduced almost but not quite (often, I think, *nicely not quite*) to vanishing point. He pulls this off in three ways. (1) Dissonant tones (like the A or F in the above example) are restricted to short note values (in modern terms crotchets or quavers). (2) They are limited to unaccented off-beats, with all strong beats kept consonant. And (3), where a suspension occurs before a cadence, a harmonically important gesture, the dissonances are still tightly restricted in length. It is worth adding that in live performance a near-sliding *portamento* can sometimes act as a further dissonance muffler, particularly on descending seconds.

Palestrina diverges from harmony, then, with the lightest of touches. As a painstaking analyst of his music put it after exhaustive observation: 'a strict yet delicate command of the dissonant element not equalled in any other epoch' (2). Suspensions and passing dissonances are less frequent than with other composers of the period, and more discreet. The discords form tiny brush strokes on the large musical canvas, facilitating the continuum of consonance, setting it in relief but no more. The dissonances are like evanescent pieces of foam in a wide-flowing river.

GRACEFUL MUTUALITY

A choir director once commented to me that singing or listening to Palestrina made him 'feel happy' not just sporadically but consistently, and some singers have said much the same. I believe that this experience of contentment can be widely shared and that it has much to do with a further feature. On top of his strict control of dissonance Palestrina adds some devices which, whatever their artistic intention or technical uses, have the effect of enhancing a sense of graceful cordiality and friendship between the parts. These devices are ubiquitous so it becomes easy to take them for granted.

First, the distribution of note values. Palestrina's use of long note values is more marked in his Mass settings, reflecting a solemnity regarded as appropriate for worship (though quavers can be vividly active at the margins, as we will find). The result is a sense of qualities which are important for good personal and social relationships, namely seriousness, reliability, steadfastness. Next, gentle gradation or stepwise sequences. Intervals of a second or third are the norm, fourths or fifths less frequent: octaves are extremely rare at least within a continuous phrase, while sevenths or greater leaps are absent. This contributes further to a sense of gentle movement. The micro-progressions have a Tao Chi quality of gentle bodily motion, also conducive to graceful interaction between the parts.

If good human and social relationships require flexibility and sensitivity, contributing to this is a further Palestrina feature, his rhythmic freedom. Also relevant is his vocal mediation: the absence of stark changes between high and low and a tendency for the middle voices to continue through successive redeployments, thereby softening changes and avoiding sharp corners.

Given all these features, it becomes inadequate to regard the lead motive when first sounded as a mere announcement, let alone a command. Rather, it can be heard as an appeal for cooperation. The ensuing responses get going even before the statement ends. Thus some sort of magnetism or *charisma* seems to be present in the opening statement. In the case of *stretto,* where imitation or variation are particularly compressed, the agreement follows quickly. By contrast, variation can be heard as more diverse convergences so that the cooperative responses seem like 'We agree but wish to put it differently, in our own way', or 'we arrive at the same idea from a different angle'.

Elastic, less structured counterpoint adds a further dimension. There the voices seem to be saying 'Yes, but here is a further implication', or 'Yes, but the idea takes us to a different point' or 'let's see what more we can make of it'. If thematically structured counterpoint can be heard as amicable yet purposive exchange, dialogue or 'ideal conversation', elastic counterpoint seems akin to convivial companionship or enjoyment at 'just being together'.

In these ways Palestrina tends to excel his leading contemporaries, whatever their contrasting merits. Orlando di Lasso's music leans towards more frequent dissonance, a less reliable pulse, an intriguing restlessness. Tomas Luis de Victoria employs more chordalism. Despite its likeness to Palestrina's, Victoria's counterpoint edges more towards the major/minor, 'happy *versus* sad' tonal system. In the music of another Renaissance giant, William Byrd, there is more dissonance and rhythmic variety, and a more dramatic involvement with detailed textual changes. These add to the interest, along with a lesser role for clear, configuring melody, and one might say, as with Lassus, less reliability and continuity. Indeed, Byrd's admirers see such features as part of his genius alongside his great imaginativeness and versatility.

To all this should be added a marked contrast with these other composers in terms of sheer volume of output. Palestrina benefited from greater professional security through most of his career, his Roman-Petrine status, a fuller body of publications and, not least, the advantage of a longer life span. So in overall terms he produces a greater amount of the counterpoint to which he was so consistently devoted, its social symbolism extending over a much wider canvas.

Footnotes

(1) For example, Nicholas Cook applies the term 'conversation' to some Mozart chamber music, Hermann Scherchen describes a Bach organ prelude as 'the joint meditation of a community', Schweitzer expresses similar ideas about Bach's music in wider terms, Edmund Rubbra explicitly pursued in his own music ideas of 'conversation', 'discourse' or 'dialogue'.

(2) Knud Jeppesen, *The Style of Palestrina and the Dissonance*, 1946, reprinted by Dover Publications, New York, 2005, 11.

Chapter 6

'The Quality of Mercy': *Kyrie Eleison*

Palestrina's record-breaking engagement with the Mass began in the 1550s. During this early phase in his career he was struggling and experimenting. He was able to pore over manuscripts of other composers' works in the Sistine Chapel. Secular music took up much of his time. His Mass settings were heavily retrospective and derivative, strongly influenced by Franco-Flemish predecessors. They tended to be schematic, sometimes stilted, and relatively few have been recorded.

The early Masses *Ecce Sacerdos Magnus* and *Benedicta es* employed an old fashioned priority for a single voice part within the polyphony, the cantus fermus. *Benedicta es* used a work by the 15th century master Josquin des Pres as a model. An unusually long setting, it features a sinuous, arguably over-elaborate melodic lead. One is tempted to hear it as a young man 'trying too hard'. Another relatively early work, the Mass *Ut re mi fa sol la,* scored unusually for CCAATB, displays an almost nerdish virtuosity. Inspired by the hexachord or six note scale, it is full of scalic phrases of varying lengths and note values, upward climbing or descending like so many small ladders: a linear, rectangular format which allows little room for balancing curves or graceful interactions. Pursued through all six sections of the Mass, the result is intriguing, though angular, rather jagged and unduly repetititive, perhaps more interesting for singers and students than typical listeners.

By the mid-1560s, his status and prospects more secure, Palestrina was increasingly finding his own voice (chapter 2). Two Mass settings, the elaborate *Missa Papae Marcelli* and the more compact *Missa Brevis,* already display a compositional brilliance combined with fitness for worship that later Mass settings would hardly excel. Abandoning backward looking derivation and highly structured melodic formats, both fell into the category of largely free ranging, elastic counterpoint. This early middle period also brought a plethora of motets and other works containing rich material which he would plunder and elaborate in later Mass settings.

After 1570, which saw the publication of a third book of Masses, the timing of his Mass compositions becomes notoriously hard to pin down on account of long delays in publication due to shortages of funds. Many years could elapse before a completed Mass got published. Various factors suggest a relative downturn in output during the 1570s. The loss of his brother Silla and his sons Rodolfo and Angelo were major tragedies (chapter 2). By the late 1570s, at the request of Gregory X111, Palestrina was struggling with a formidable project to revise and simplify the huge legacy of plainchant inherited by the Church through the centuries. This proved to be a labyrinthine task he was unable to complete. He was also composing a special category of bespoke Masses, alternating plainchant and polyphony, for Duke Guglielmo of Mantua (see chapter 7). However, after the massive upheavals in 1580-81 – trauma following the death of Lucrezia, moves towards the priesthood, marriage to Virginia, greater financial security and new business activities – a new phase of renewed creativity opened up. Palestrina's health seems to have reflected a strong constitution and he survived until the age of 68. Many of his finest Masses seem to have been composed during the 1580s and early 1590s.

Leaving aside the largely experimental early period, does it matter that overall stages of development, a favourite concept for scholars, are hard to identify ? I suggest, not much. A high degree of continuity is apparent from the 1560s onwards. A handful of polychoral Masses, published much later, though slightly anticipating the Baroque with larger singing numbers and dramatic chordal antiphonies, were less than mould-breaking. Palestrina's habit of developing material from earlier (often much earlier) compositions contributed to a bridging effect between the different periods. Perhaps most important were the continuities as he returned repeatedly to the unchanging format of the Latin Mass. Its texts, progressions and mystique remained constant through the late 16th century (just as they have, in the main, remained constant ever since).

Readers should be warned about some confusing terminology. One classification of the Masses focusses on the melodic leads which appear in most of them, leading to implications about entire compositional processes. Where the source is a piece of chant or a popular song a favoured term is 'paraphrase Mass'. Where the format develops out of a pre-existing polyphonic work (another composer's or Palestrina's) the term 'parody Mass' is used. These labels do less than justice to his creativity. Similarly when the terms 'imitation' or 'imitative' are applied in blanket fashion to both of these categories. As for the less structured, more elastic settings, those which lack recurring melodic material, often these are described as 'free composed', rather awkwardly implying that the foregoing categories were somehow copycat or constricted.

It is important to understand that each section of the Mass has its own text, liturgical role, devotional purposes and symbolic potential. Soaked as he was in the detail of the Mass since his early days as a boy chorister, Palestrina would approach each one with an eye to continuity but also with differing ideas. The section-by-section approach I adopt in the following chapters should make things easier for readers unfamiliar with the Latin and the church ceremonial. It should also help readers who may wish to dip into a Mass recording selectively, approaching it bit-by-bit rather than trying to imbibe the whole thing in a single gulp.

'A FOUNTAIN AMONG RIVULETS'

Passionate feelings about the Mass were at a zenith among late 16th century Catholics (chapter 2). Palestrina may well have looked up the relevant ideas in the authoritative *Catechism of the Council of Trent,* first published in 1566. This declared that a sacrament was 'a holy thing that lies concealed and hidden', 'a visible sign of an invisible grace'. It was a special aid to personal salvation, a cause of the unity of believers, and above all an objective divine action, 'effecting what it signifies'. Sacraments were instituted, according to the *Catechism,* partly because human weakness needed material objects as a practical starting-point towards spiritual things. They would also be exercises in humility 'for they oblige us to subject ourselves to sensible elements in obedience to God' (1).

The *Catechism* insisted on the *primacy* of the Mass among the sacraments: it was 'a fountain', the others 'rivulets'. Careful preparation and examination of conscience were essential. Daily communion was desirable, yearly communion at Easter obligatory. Emphasis on the Real Presence of Christ was central. The bread and wine after consecration were 'truly the substance of the body and blood of Christ', 'the flesh and blood of our Lord Jesus Christ Himself', 'dependant not on the merit of the minister'. They came as an unconditional gift, although the benefits would depend on the receiver's piety and the extent of follow-up through good works as well as faith.

The reality of Christ's presence in the transformed elements of bread and wine had long been a core belief, regarded as divinely mandated by the scriptural account of Christ's promise at the Last Supper. Catholics were shocked by what they saw (often through the lens of highly biassed propaganda on their own side) as Protestant dilutions, denials or desecrations. How could the Real Presence be reduced to mere remembrance, instruction or intransitive symbol, let alone mocked or insulted ? Invoking the early Fathers and centuries of tradition, the Council of Trent had reaffirmed the doctrine of *transubstantiation:* a sea change in the bread and wine once consecrated, a formula drawing on the Aristotelian-scholastic distinction between 'accident' (appearance) and 'substance' (reality).

The doctrine was being widely re-emphasised through Palestrina's life. Teresa of Avila wrote about Christ's unconditional generosity in the Sacrament, especially to the sinner. Employing a pungent symbol which referred in the first instance to the fraction and distribution of the consecrated Host before communion, in a wider sense to a divine love all too often rejected or ignored, Teresa suggested that Christ was carrying the gift of Himself in the consecrated wafer to the point of 'allowing himself to be crushed to pieces every day'. She was not alone in seeing thanksgiving and adoration after communion as central for the spiritual life.

The cult of frequent communion was enjoined in a series of widely circulating devotional books between the 1550s and the 1590s. It was a core obligation for members of the fast-growing lay confraternities, including the SS Trinita to which Palestrina belonged. A further spin-off, apart from the Mass itself, was the practice of regular exposition and adoration of the Sacrament on the altar. In a new devotion, the *Quarant'ore*, the Eucharist was being displayed and revered in this way for forty hours, symbolising the time of Christ's sojourn in the grave between his death and resurrection.

Not that worldliness ever could disappear. In Rome regular Mass going could include aesthetic pleasure, enjoyment of the music, display of respectability, the satisfaction of mingling with the powerful, an opportunity to be seen as well as to see. Some of the attending dignitaries would be involved in nepotism, closet sexuality or power struggles within the papal court. Montaigne would comment acidly on the sight of cardinals chattering inattentively at Mass in Saint Peter's on Christmas Day in1582. The grotesque abuses of the pre-Reformation papacy were largely a thing of the past, but an old adage would linger in the Catholic world, *veduta Roma, perduta fede,* 'once you've seen Rome, you've lost your faith'.

For many centuries popular religion had drawn liberally on physical symbols, some with pagan antecedents. These could be more meaningful for people than sermons or reading material. In contrast to a Protestant insistence on the centrality of scripture reading and 'the Word', the Catholic Reform, though also keen on preaching, was clear that people were more likely to internalise the faith if it was enacted by tangible sacrament through varied feast days and holidays, with the aid of icons, wall paintings, gestures and processions. And music would be a vital part of the mix.

SIGNIFICANCE OF THE *KYRIE*

The text of the first section of a choral Mass, the *Kyrie*, is brief – just the words *Kyrie eleison, Christe eleison, Kyrie eleison,* 'Lord have mercy, Christ have mercy, Lord have mercy' - but it is highly charged with concepts of God. The compact text, combined with a spun-out musical treatment, helps to focus our attention on total sound, melody, rhythm, voice deployment and contrapuntal form. Most of the *Kyrie* sections involve listening for between three and five minutes, making them ideal for a sampling of Palestrina's music.

In the now exceptional Tridentine liturgy, following the entry procession, the celebrant has moved around sprinkling people with holy water to the text *Asperges me,* 'Thou shalt sprinkle me, O Lord, with hyssop, and I will be cleansed: Thou shalt wash me, and I will be made whiter than snow'. A constant in formats both new and old is a general confession, the *Confiteor,* in which the congregation collectively confess their sins to God, Mary, the Saints and each other, and ask for pardon. Choral music now makes its first big entry. The words recall a Greek strand in the history of the Church alongside its largely Hebraic roots (earlier a longer litany had included congregational responses). At this point choral singing becomes central so that during its performance nothing else is going on. Hence there is an opportunity to 'interiorise' what has been said and done so far, which the music needs to assist and promote.

Palestrina nearly always treats the three invocations, *Kyrie eleison, Christe eleison, Kyrie eleison,* as sub-sections. Often he reduces the number of parts in the *Christe* sub-section. In the *Christe,* too, choir directors sometimes opt for fewer singers and slightly slower tempi. The cantus singers mostly initiate the melodic lead in *Kyrie 1,* whereas in the *Christe* and *Kyrie 2* sub-sections it is generally the middle or lower parts that start things off. After its initial sounding by one or more parts, the lead is successively taken up by the others until all are involved (chapter 3). Often there is greater complexity. Either the melodic lead goes alongside *other* melodic-rhythmic lines so its role is harder to recognise. Alternatively, there are *two* or sometimes even *three* themes virtually from the start, each involving varied assortments of voice parts.

The following illustration shows the starting phrases of the *Kyrie* in the *Missa Papae Marcelli,* the showpiece work which attracted senior Catholic dignitaries with striking effects on Palestrina's standing and which has intrigued admirers ever since.

Looking carefully, one begins to understand how this entry could have enticed them from the start. Notice the slow single note drumbeat rhythm on the word *Kyrie* in all the voice parts, followed by the upward tilts on *eleison*. Interest builds up as this phrase gets repeated two or three times by every voice part until all six are involved. There is a mounting sense of solemnity and deliberation as the acoustic space fills up. Notice also the overlaps and staggerings. Neither rhythmic nor syllabic unison is evident. The parts sing all together only at the start of bar 9 and the start of bar 12, but even then their syllables differ. A characteristic of the whole work is already evident: an onward moving, broadly unifying sweep as of

[Musical score: Missa Papae Marcelli, Kyrie]

a whole river, but within this a multitude of micro ebbs-and-flows darting back and forth.

DIVERSITIES AND EQUALITIES

In the last chapter I outlined core features of Palestrina's counterpoint which converge so as to symbolise good social relationships or ideal community. Two of these features, differentiation of voice parts and equality between the parts, can be observed in his settings of the *Kyrie*.

To start with the differentiation, analysis of seven Masses in my core sample showed 124 cases where a melodic lead or leads, after appearing at the start of the *Kyrie*, went on to reappear in its later phases. Only in 23 cases were these precise copies of the original. In a further 22 cases they were augmentations or diminutions. There were as many as 79 diversifications. The small 'heads' of the melodic lead or leads got shorter 'tails' added to them (29 cases). Alternatively, more interestingly, the 'heads' sprouted longer 'tails' (50 cases).

	Table Y					
	Seven *Kyrie* settings: developments of melodic leads					
	No of such developments	Precise imitations	Diminutions	Augmentations	Same heads with	
					different & shorter tails	different & longer tails
Dies Sanctificatus	31	4	5	2	8	12
Missa Brevis	19	4	1	1	3	5
O Sacrum Convivum	19	3	1	-	8	7
Aeterna Christi Munera	16	2	2	2	3	7
Ascendo ad Patrem	15	2	1	1	1	10
Sine Nomine a 4	12	3	-	-	4	5
O Rex Gloriae	12	5	1	-	2	4
Totals	124	23	16	6	29	50

That variation easily outstrips exact duplication should be unsurprising. Composing in counterpoint demands a flexibility which slavish imitation will disfavour. Also repeated duplication could easily become boring. However, my point just now is that as a melodic lead far more typically gets played around with - sometimes to a point of tenuous resemblance to the original - so the voice parts have lines even more specifically their own; that is, in addition to their different pitches and their variable entry and exit points.

The following illustration shows in detail in two *Kyrie* sections, those belonging to the Masses *Dies Sanctificatus* and *Viri Galilei*, what Palestrina does with a melodic lead and how quickly the voice parts strike out on different paths.

The *Christe* sub-section of the *Kyrie* in the *Missa Dies Sanctificatus*, shows the starting melodic lead going through various twists and turns despite a basic family likeness (points 1-7). By point 7 there is a precise return to the simplified theme at point 2, showing a certain symmetricality. Part of the interest here lies in the micro-individuality which emerges even in a relatively structured and disciplined Mass setting. By contrast, in the *Kyrie 1* sub-section of *Viri Galilei,* one of Palestrina's less structured and more elastic settings, the varieties are a lot more striking. Indeed, the original theme almost gets lost. These sorts of pattern, either neatly contoured or free ranging, can be repeatedly observed in Palestrina's motets and in the Mass settings, but always showing individuality in the voice parts.

As to equality between the voice parts, a purely quantitative measure is available: the percentage of total bars sung by each part. The following table applies this measure to 12 *Kyrie* sections. No great difference emerges between the cantus, alto and tenor parts (though the altos emerge by a short head as the most active). The basses are the least fully employed. Random checks broadly confirmed this ordering across the whole field of Mass settings.

'The Quality of Mercy': Kyrie Eleison

Development of melodic leads

Christe eleison in Missa Dies Sanctificatus

1. Tenors initiate theme
2. Basses follow but simplify & shorten 'tail'
3. Cantus almost precisely imitate basses
4. Altos almost completely follow
5. Basses almost completely modify
6. Altos follow bass 'head' but offer new & longer 'tail'
7. Cantus return to 2 above

Kyrie I in Missa Viri Galilei

1. Altos (1) initiate theme
2. Altos (2) follow 'head' but offer new 'tail'
3. Basses almost completely modify
4. Tenors also substantially modify
5. Cantus drastically reduce

Percentage of bars sung by each part in 12 *Kyrie* sections				
	Cantus	Alto	Tenor	Bass
Highest	90%	96%	96%	83%
Lowest	75%	76%	73%	51%
¾ majority above	83%	86%	84%	70%

However, a more qualitative measure is available. Equality implies that each voice part should contribute fully to key phrases of text and where more importantly, we might think, than in appeals to or namings of God ? Diagram Y below provides relevant data for the 12 *Kyrie* sections already mentioned. Each X represents a percentage share of the invocations *Kyrie eleison, Christe eleison,* and of cases where the single words *Kyrie, eleison* or *Christe* extend through a melodic phrase, the nodal point for strict equality being 25 %. What emerges is indeed a pattern of roughly equal sharing. Although the altos are more likely to exceed 25 % than the basses, the large bulk of the sacred invocations bring all voice parts within a few percentage points of 25 %. This pattern is typical also in Palestrina's motets and in later movements of the Mass, notably at similar invocations of the Most High on the words *Sanctus* and *Agnus Dei*.

Percentage shares of invocations among parts

Percentages	Cantus	Altos	Tenors	Basses
30				
29		x x x x	x x	
28		x x		
27	x x x x			
26	x x x x	x x	x x	x x x x
25		x x x x	x x x x x	
24	x x	x x	x x x x x	x x
23	x x		x	x x
22		x x	x x x	x x
21	x x x x	x x	x x x x	x x x x x
20	x x	x x	x x x	
19	x x x x x	x x x x	x x x x	
18		x x x x x x	x	x
17	x x		x x	x
16	x		x x	x x x
15	x			x
14				x x
13				x

'GENTLE DEW FROM HEAVEN'

'The mercy of God goes before us and converts our hearts to him' …'To recall a sinner from the state of sin to that of righteousness is even a greater work than to create the heavens and earth from nothing' …'Forgiveness proclaims the ineffable Providence of God and the abundance of His love for us'. Thus spoke the *Catechism* of 1566. On the one hand, there was the gravity and pervasiveness of sin, 'the frailty and weakness of human nature'; on the other, 'the infinite power of God', 'His infinite goodness and mercy'.

You do not have to be a Christian to appreciate the music that tries to intimate these realms. They can be entered vicariously, historically or imaginatively by atheists, agnostics or freewheelers. Emotional, visual or socio-symbolic values can be drawn from them. Wider terms than 'mercy' can be chosen for them: *forgiveness, kindness, generosity, magnanimity, forbearance, compassion*. Or the terms of Portia's plea to Shylock in *The Merchant of Venice*:

> The quality of mercy is not strained;
> It droppeth as the gentle rain from heaven
> Upon the place beneath. It is twice blest:
> It blesseth him that gives and him that takes.

Many people nowadays may find some of the 1566 *Catechism* surprising. Hell gets little attention. The commandment 'Thou shalt not steal' is much dwelt on (with condemnations of exploiting the poor and of 'usury', though the latter prohibition had become largely theoretical). 'Satisfaction' or 'offering to God some reparation' implies prayer, fasting and 'almsdeeds', the last interpreted as 'generosity and kindness to the poor and needy'. Restitution and 'public penance for public sins' might be required. The emotional extremes of complacency and pessimism are warned against. Repentance should be profound and sincere, but faith, hope and the love of God were to prevail over undue sorrow, fear or anxiety (2).

Palestrina had significant contact with the new, increasingly influential Jesuit order, commando troops of the Counter Reformation. For several years he taught music in their new higher education college, the Seminario Romano, where his sons Rodolfo and Angelo were pupils. He was probably familiar with *The Spiritual Exercises* of the order's founder, Ignatius Loyola, a work widely read at the time. Advocating personal disciplines of examination of conscience, repentance and daily tabulation of sins and lapses, the *Exercises* focussed on slow motion, lively and imaginative reflections on the successive events of Christ's life.

A final comment. The *Kyries* of some later composers would emphasise sadness, grief for sin, sorrowful pleas to God. In doing so they would be helped by the resources of mainstream tonality, by stable minor keys, sometimes by chromatics. In this category come the relatively sombre *Kyries in* Mozart's C Minor Mass and his *Requiem Mass*, in Haydn's 'Nelson' and *Pauken* Masses, and perhaps most strikingly of all in J.S. Bach's B Minor Mass or Verdi's *Requiem*.

By contrast, Palestrina's *Kyries* do not come across as particularly sorrowful, anguished or beseeching. Such moods are more prominent in some of his motets, for example *Super flumina Babylonis* or *Tribulationes civitatum,* or in much of his Holy Week music (chapter 4). His *Kyries* do not express anguish or a sense of lying prostrate before the Almighty, weighed down by grief and contrition. It was this which doubtless led Saint Saens, a leading critic, to express impatience with the *Kyrie* in the *Missa Papae Marcelli*: 'Wherein does {it} express supplication ? Here is nothing else but form' . Clearly, Saint Saens felt cheated of some representation of subjective human emotion probably in 'pictorial' form (3).

A different sort of contrast emerges with upbeat moods in other settings. Here one thinks of *Kyries* that are radiant or exuberant, notably in Haydn's *Harmoniemesse*, in Mozart's C major Mass, or in a whole string of Schubert's Masses (in F, B flat, C, A flat and

E flat major). If it were not for their compositional brilliance, the joyfulness we hear in these works might almost seem too easily expressed through the use of stable major keys. But however they were heard in his own time, joyfulness is not what mostly strikes us today in Palestrina's largely white note modal *Kyries*. Once more we face ambiguities, pulling us away from obvious drama, hinting at subtler readings.

A greater contrast arises with monumentalism. Palestrina's *Kyries* convey a different ethos from *en masse* polychoralism as in Giovanni Gabrieli or the 'colossal Baroque' of a Maximilian Biber. They are still more distant from Beethoven and Brahms in their mighty concert-orientated, non-liturgical Masses (4). For Palestrina's *Kyries* are relatively brief. They do not overshadow pulpit or altar. They do not come across as triumphalist, assertive or pressuring.

Saint Saens misunderstood the priority here. The belief is that God, the Source of prayer, actuates the asking ('His mercy goes before us'), with the implication that a continued harping on human need and emotion would be anthropocentric or self-absorbed. It would be easy for listeners to get stuck on the subjective human meanings, forgetting the transcendent mystery that lies inside as a gift from God. Some lines of Robert Frost seem apposite.

> 'Beware of coming too much to the surface
> And using for apparel what was meant
> To be the curtain of the inmost soul' (5)

Footnotes

(1) *Catechism of the Council of Trent,* 1566, edited under Charles Borromeo and published by decree of Pope Pius V, Part 2, *The Sacraments*.

(2) *Catechism, op cit, The Mass*.

(3) Camille Saint-Saens, in *Outspoken Essays,* cited in Henry Coates, *Palestrina,* London 1938, 81.

(4) Bach's Lutheran Masses are in a different category, being restricted to the *Kyrie* and *Gloria,* and greatly expanding those sections. His vast, inimitable B Minor Mass was not intended for regular liturgical use.

(5) Robert Frost, *The Fear of God.*

Chapter 7

Gloria and Credo

Two of the choral Mass's longest and most complex texts, the *Gloria* and the *Credo,* would pose major challenges for Palestrina. Large numbers of words had to be accommodated, far more than in the other sections of the Mass: 79 in the *Gloria,* 160 in the *Credo.* In the *Gloria* the music would need to adjust to significant changes of mood and meaning, although the momentum of the text and its lively contrasts would repeatedly find their match in Palestrina's resourcefulness.

The *Credo* was more complex. Here are tight textual summaries of complex, interlocking beliefs Christianity had accumulated through its early centuries. Although Palestrina is more compact than many other composers of Masses, his *Credos* typically take six, seven or eight minutes to sing through, making them difficult to accommodate on top of much other music in the liturgy. Musical treatments of the tightly packed formulas can easily emerge as barebones skeletal or else over-elaborate. Even here there is a case for thinking that Palestrina exhibits much that is ingenious and exemplary, However, it is hard to claim that his *Credo* renderings represent the best of his work. It is at this point, too, that long standing questions come to a head about the role of full scale choral music within the liturgy.

In Palestrina's time and in later periods complete choral *Credos* would fit nicely in the context of lengthy, elaborate High Masses, particularly on major feast days and in leading basilicas with professional choirs. In modern times such conditions have become much less common. For complex reasons liturgical performance of a full scale polyphonic *Credo* has receded, also of the *Gloria*. Time constraints and shortages of trained singers help to explain this. Added to which there has always been a case for these sections to be less elaborate. Chant may be preferable to full-scale choralism, some congregational participation may be appropriate.

ACCLAMATION, ENCOUNTER, CLIMACTIC AFFIRMATION

After the gentle atmosphere of the *Kyrie* the *Gloria* quickly follows with a burst of energy. One of Christianity's most ancient hymns, it features regularly within church liturgies (except during the seasons of Advent and Lent when more restrained styles of music have been preferred). Originally the *Gloria* was probably chanted by congregations. Later on clerics and monastic communities would sing it regularly in more elaborate plainchant, while later still virtuoso composers would include it in their full-scale choral settings of the Mass. The text proceeds in three stages: praise and acclamation, then encounter with God's mercy, and finally a climactic affirmation of the divine being.

The acclaiming first section goes as follows:

Gloria in excelsis Deo: et in terra pax hominibus bonae voluntatis.	Glory be to God on high and on earth peace to men of goodwill.
Laudamus te, benedicimus te, adoramus te,	We praise Thee, we bless Thee, we adore
glorificamus te. Gratias agimus tibi propter magnam gloriam tuam.	Thee. We glorify Thee. We give Thee Thanks for Thy great glory.

Domine Deus, Rex coelestis, Deus Pater	Lord God, heavenly King, almighty God
Omnipotens. Domine Fili unigenite Jesu Christe. Domine Deus, Agnus Dei, Filius Patris.	and Father. Lord Jesus Christ, only Son of the Father. Lord God, Lamb of God Son of the Father.

After a plainchant introduction, *Gloria in excelsis Deo*, a Palestrina *Gloria* typically renders *et in terra pax hominibus bonae voluntatis* in concise, compact fashion. A sequence follows of praises of God, starting with *Laudamus te,* often with short, punchy chordal phrases. We hear the stresses on 'a' in the words *laudamus,* and *adoramus*, building up to a mini-climax on the five syllable *glorificamus*. Then come namings of the Praised One either with solemn chords or in usually close-knit counterpoint. Emphasis increases until the words *Jesu Christe* actuate mixtures of harmonic inflection, longer note values in some voice parts, quaver melismas in others. A further wave of namings from *Dominus Deus* onwards, adding gracefulness to ritual repetition, finally comes to rest on a typically beautific *Filius Patris*.

These phrases nearly always come across as rhythmically compelling and activist. One hears both praises and namings as human endeavours in face of the sublime. The energy of this first stage of the *Gloria*, its rhythmic shape and verbal stresses, has a strongly physical feel, akin to the 'gesture' suggested by Roger Scruton as a figure for human activity transferred to 'the realm of pure sound' (1). A Palestrina *Gloria* seems to enlist us physically, vicariously, rather as if we are joining the statues of saints along the aisles of a church, exclaiming, exhorting, gesticulating towards God. Then come the phrases of encounter.

Qui tollis peccata mundi, miserere nobis	You who take away the sins of the world, have
Qui tollis peccata mundi, suscipe deprecationem nostram. Qui sedes ad dexteram Patris, miserere nobis.	mercy on us. You who take away the sins of the the world, receive our prayer. You who sit at the right hand of the Father, have mercy on us.

Palestrina nearly always prefaces these phrases with a pause. Often he further emphasises a gear change by shifting from counterpoint to a spasm of homophony. Having praised and invoked Christ in relation to the Father, the text now addresses God more directly. The music slightly relaxes. A chordal structure gets looser or counterpoint returns with occasional touches of homophony usually involving all the voice parts, notably on the word *suscipe*. This section can be experienced as a letting go, a more reflective, intimate trusting in the Lord. Contemporary performers sometimes moderate both tempo and dynamics, though such restraint can slide easily towards the timid or tepid. Then finally comes invocation of the divine being *per se* as follows.

Quoniam tu solus sanctus, tu solus	For you alone are holy, you alone are the Lord, you
Sanctus, Tu solus altissimus, Jesu Christe, cum Sancto Spiritu, in gloria Dei Patris, Amen.	alone are the most high, Jesus Christ, with the Holy Spirit, in the glory of God the Father, Amen.

Quite often Palestrina marks this shift by once again moving briefly to homophony, quickly followed by a reversion to counterpoint. The initial *quoniam* tends to be crisply businesslike. The core sample of 32 Masses shows a strong preference for elastic rather than highly structured counterpoint in this final section. The sequence works particularly well, for instance, in the *Missa Papae Marcelli,* and in the *Ave Maria a 4*. Sometimes, too, there are moves to triple time. Quaver runs sometimes reach an apex of joyful fluidity round the words *Jesu Christe* and *Gloria*. Voice registers often spin out to their respective highs or lows on these runs while inter-part staggerings typically make for splendid cross rhythms.

Even in the midst of Palestrina's most impressive Masses these phrases stand out. I would particularly single out the sustained treatments in *Hodie Christus natus est* (where the two choir antiphony makes for great excitement), also in *Tu es Petrus, Sicut lilium, O*

Gloria and Credo 99

Sacrum Convivium and *Dum Complerentur,* but there are many others. The build-up in the penultimate phrases of the *Gloria* in the Mass *O Rex Gloriae,* shown below, provides a vivid illustration.

These final sections emanate a sense of God's being as generous outflow. Shortly before the end a climax is suggested by a larger-than-usual macro-rhythm, usually combined with high notes, but this declines to a lesser wave that finishes, as it were, with a gentle lap on the shore. The *Amens* typically combine dynamism and rest: one or two moving parts *plus* multiple breves or semi-breves elsewhere in the texture. The slim triad endings avoid a massive, definitive crunch. They can be interpreted as tapering off with a sense of on-goingness, perhaps intimating something of the eternity as well as infinity of God.

PALESTRINA'S CREDOS: A SKELETAL OUTLINE

The *Credo*, far and away the longest section of the regular choral Mass, differs radically in character from the other sections. Its text affirms a hallowed corpus of Christian belief stemming back to the resolution of doctrinal disputes at the Councils of Nicea in 325 AD and Constantinople in 381 AD. Its statements, particularly about Christ's nature as both human and divine - and about the Trinity - are fundamental for mainstream Christianity.

Whereas other texts in the Mass praise God, seek to move towards Him or intimate the divine attributes, the text of the *Credo* is essentially propositional and, as it stands on the naked page, seemingly pedagogic. Some clauses invoke eternal truths, others tell of divine actions in history, still others flag up implications of all this including forgiveness of sins, an historic, ongoing Church, and life everlasting. Interdependences between many of the clauses, both syntactical and theological, add still further complexity.

Here are the opening phrases.

Credo in unum Deum, Patrem omnipotentem,	I believe in one God, the Father Almighty,
Factorem coeli et terrae, visibilium omnium et invisibilium.	Maker of heaven and earth, and of all things visible and invisible.

Et in unum Dominum Jesum Christum,	And in one Lord Jesus Christ, the only
Filium Dei unigenitum.	begotten Son of God.
Et ex Patre natum ante omnia saecula.	Born of the Father before all ages.
Deum de Deo, lumine de lumine, Deum	God of God, Light of Light, true God
verum de Deo vero. Genitum non	of true God, begotten not made,
factum, consubstantialem Patri	consubstantial with the Father
per quem omnia facta sunt.	by whom all things were made.

After a chanted *Credo in unum Deum*, the words *Patrem Omnipotentem* often recapitulate the melodic lead introduced in *Kyrie eleison 1*. An emphasis on *invisibilium* exalts the 'invisible'. The words *Jesum Christum* tend to inspire longer note values and decorative inflection *plus* in some settings high registers in some voices, including basses and tenors, or interesting harmonic inflections (a C minor triad in the *Missa Papae Marcelli* is an example). The words *Deum de Deo* etc, nicely shaped for semi-repetition, insist on Christ's generation from and equality with the Father, typically arriving at a stronger emphasis on *Deum Verum de Deo Vero*.

Qui propter nos homines et propter	Who for us men and for our
nostram salutem descendit de coelis.	salvation came down from heaven.
Et incarnatus est de Spiritu Sancto	And was incarnate by the Holy Spirit
ex Maria Virgine,	of the Virgin Mary,
et homo factus est.	and was made man.

Here we come to the core salvation narrative. The words *descendit de coelis* tempt one to expect a downward move in the music, but this is far from clear or universal. Fortunately so for neither musical nor theological criteria would particularly favour it (2). The move to *et incarnatus est* is invariably preceded by a pause, usually a minim rest, a very rare moment of silence. Then comes an impactful change, a move from counterpoint to homophony in as many as 56 of the Mass settings. This makes for solemnity, the words being framed within a drawn-out, chordal phrase usually involving all the voice parts. The sub-phrase *ex Maria Virgine* usually takes a beautifully graceful turn with gentle embellishment. It seems right for performances of the whole phrase to fall back to *adagio* speed.

Crucifixus etiam pro nobis sub Pontio Pilato,	He was crucified also for us under Pontius Pilate,
Passus et sepultus est.	He died and was buried.

These words often bring a reverse move from homophony to counterpoint. Listen to *Aeterna Christi Munera, Assumpta est Maria*, the *Missa Brevis, Papae Marcelli, O Rex Gloriae, Sicut Lilium*, for example, and you will hear a change from solemn mainly chordal sequences to a thinner texture, linear, sinuous and austere. Typically, fewer voices sing an imitative, tight-knit counterpoint, and the effect can be almost desolating as each part weighs in with more or less the same sighing phrase. Sometimes there is a tilt to lower voices in this passage, but mostly to higher ones, the latter offering a touch of stark acidity.

A minor point is the enticing rhythm of the words *sub Pontio Pilato*. In many settings these words receive a slight emphasis, maybe trivial except that it serves to bring out the earthly grounding of Christ's sacrifice in human time and context. A more important issue arises over dissonance. The doyen of 20th century Palestrina musicologists, Knud Jeppesen, expected the tragic phrases to be emotionally intensified by dissonances, as often happens with later composers. But after much laborious sifting he found only occasional cases (3).

Et resurrexit tertia die secundum Scripturas. Et ascendit in coelum, sedet ad dexteram Patris.	And the third day He rose again according to the Scriptures. And ascended into heaven and sits at the right hand of the Father.
Et iterum venturus est cum gloria Judicare vivos et mortuos;	And He will come again with glory to judge the living and the dead,
cujus regni non erit finis.	And his kingdom will have no end.

At the mighty turning-point on *et resurrexit* we return with striking effect to shorter note values, often with strong rhythms or quaver runs. Palestrina's scoring of the second most focal phrase for Christianity, *et resurrexit tertia die secondum Scripturas,* tends to run to the equivalent of five to ten bars, but the rest is brisker. In 13 settings in the whole opus of Mass settings he moves to triple time. In this clause the lower voices are sometimes used to great effect (examples occur in *Aeterna Christi Munera*, the *Missa Brevis, Ecce ego sum Joannes* and the *Missa Papae Marcelli*).

The crudely spatial metaphor on *et ascendit* tempts one to expect a copycat upward figure in the music, but as with the *descendit* phrase a fleeting treatment and contrapuntal staggering reduce the chance of this making a mark. Also the sheer musical frequency of ascending figures would trivialise such a gesture (4). At *cujus regni non erit finis* one thinks of the marvellous 20 bars of *ritornelli* at this point in Bach's B minor Mass. Palestrina comes nowhere near such repetition, though he tends to intimate eternity round the words *non erit finis* in ways that seldom disappoint.

Et in Spiritum Sanctum, Dominum et Vivificantem, qui ex Patre Filioque procedit. Qui cum Patre et Filio simul adoratur et conglorificatur: qui locutus est per Prophetas.	And in the Holy Spirit, the Lord and Giver of Life, Who proceeds from the Father and the Son. Who with the Father and the Son together is glorified: Who spoke through the Prophets.

This passage is distinguished by occasional resort to triple time, emphases on the word *vivificantem*, symbolising the quickening power of the Spirit, and frequent plays on the word *conglorificatur*, stressing the Holy Spirit's co-equality and co-eternity with the Father and Son. Frequently, 'punctuating' moves to homophony add impact. The words *qui locutus est per Prophetas* sometimes give strong, athletic play to the basses within the vocal texture.

Et in unam Sanctam Catholicam et Apostolicam	And in one holy Catholic and Apostolic

Ecclesiam. Confiteor unum Baptisma in remissionem peccatorum. Et exspecto resurrectionem mortuorum. Et vitam venturi saeculi. Amen.

Church. I confess one Baptism for the remission of sins. And I look for the resurrection of the dead. And the life of the world to come. Amen.

In this final 'implications' section, beginning with *et unam sanctam Catholicam,* the pace gets relatively brisk, even rather business-like. By now a slight speed-up seems defensible. Beauty and poetry are held in reserve for the concluding phrase, *et vitam venturi saeculi, Amen.* There, in one setting after another, they summon up great depths. Richard Taruskin applies the label 'a thrilling peroration' to the *tutti* in this final phrase in the *Missa Papae Marcelli,* but the same could be said of many others.

PALESTRINA AND THE DUKE: THE MANTUAN EXCEPTIONS

Over nearly two decades Palestrina engaged in a correspondence with Duke Guglielmo of Mantua. This reveals a fair deal about his communications skills, aesthetic preferences and working methods, and the relationship with Duke Gugliemo led to the composition of ten Masses in a special category, combining plainchant and polyphony. Palestrina composed one of these in 1569, the rest during the period 1578-79. I want to finish this chapter with comments on the correspondence and on a fine example of how the plainchant-polyphony pattern in these 'Mantuan Masses' comes into its own in the *Gloria* and *Credo* sections.

First, a few words about Guglielmo. He had inherited the Mantua dukedom as a boy, following the death of his older brother. His mother had acted as regent until he came of age. There had been anxieties in the Mantuan court about his fitness for the role. He was a hunchback, unprepossessing in appearance, deficient in the assertive, martial, even macho style which had characterised many of his Gonzaga predecessors.

Although not the wealthiest of Italian princes, Guglielmo was a significant potentate and dynastically well connected, having married a Hapsburg archduchess. A fastidious aesthete, at one point he commissioned Tintoretto to contribute a set of canvases glorifying the Gonzaga dynasty. A leading achievement, dating from 1565, was a basilica dedicated to Santa Barbara, a local patron saint, which also served as a family chapel and mausoleum. It was a fine version of the early Baroque and an example of the Catholic Reform aesthetic, featuring a unified open space with acoustic advantages and a visually climactic high altar. Guglielmo was an amateur composer and well known for energetic, not always successful efforts to attract leading musicians to his court. He was also devout and much attached to a special liturgical format for the Mass, papally approved but peculiar to Mantua. This featured its own versions of traditional plainchant alternating with passages of counterpoint.

The correspondence between Palestrina and Duke Guglielmo followed a probable meeting in Rome in 1568. Guglielmo arranges a musical post for Palestrina's son Rodolfo in 1572 and seeks Palestrina's advice on musical appointments at his court. In 1583 he offers Palestrina himself a job as court composer (an idea which comes to nothing ostensibly because the composer holds out for too much money, though his reasons were probably more complex: see chapter 2). In various letters in 1578 we learn that Palestrina is employing a lute for compositional purposes; that he has stopped work on account of an illness affecting his eyesight; that he is completing a full Mass setting every ten days. We are left longing for more letters of this kind.

Palestrina dedicates various collections to the duke, and at one point mixes conventional flattery with some discreet criticism of Guglielmo's own compositions. In March 1570 he writes that 'in music you surpass those who worthily serve it as a profession', with 'beautiful workmanship, far removed from the common run'. He continues, 'I have indicated certain passages in which it seems to me that if one can do with less, the harmony will sound better'. 'Because of the dense interweavings of the imitations the words are somewhat obscured to the listeners'. The concern for beauty of sound and clarity of text sheds light on Palestrina's publicly declared aesthetic (his technical musical criteria would have been much fuller). Having got in his criticism, he quickly covers himself, 'Needless to say, your Excellency will understand these details much better than I'.

Fortunately, Palestrina did not move to Mantua. Though his music would still have travelled widely, constraints would have arisen relating to a rather isolated liturgy at Santa Barbara, a limited musical circle, the fussy rituals of court life and the provincialism, while Duke Guglielmo could well have been dictatorial and over-demanding.

However, the musical outome would be significant: as many as 10 Mass settings. The scores, buried away for centuries, endured tortuous misadventures, even risks of destruction, until a striking coup for archival research finally uncovered them in 1950. These 'Mantuan Masses' possess the special character of being *alternatim* Masses with large parts alternating between plainchant and polyphony. Palestrina uses ultra-simple syllabic or psalmodic plainchant in forms apparently selected and sometimes modified by Guglielmo, probably with some expert help. The longer passages of polyphony, employing five parts CATTB, conform to the traditional modes used in the chant and often incorporate their melodic lines, usually in augmented forms.

One of the masses, *In duplicibus minoribus 11*, is worth singling out. Its *Kyrie* section includes imitations around a melodic lead which starts with balancing phrases between ascending and descending fourths while a top voice *cantus fermus* augments the preceding chant, a feature which persists through later sections. There are cogent build-ups through the *Gloria* praises and towards the word *omnipotens*. Divine inter-relations are fluidly intimated in the section

Dominus Deus ....Filius Patris. The *Credo* features a lower voice emphasis on *et ex Patre natum* and parallel quaver phrases on *ex Maria Virgine*. The *alternatim* style means that the *Gloria* and the *Credo*, though not specially elaborate, take the best part of 20 minutes to perform. The *Credo* features as many as 19 moves between slivers of plainchant and brief polyphonic episodes.

There is a certain enchantment in this contrast. The plainchant shows a steady, calm insistence while the polyphonic sections, though too short for their musical ideas to develop, deliver fine counterpoint in jewel-like microcosms. Brief silences between the two add to the interest. What seems to emerge in the *Credo* is a reflective, prayerful rendering of the articles of faith, perhaps suitable for accompanying exercises in meditation.

It seems appropriate, then, to salute Palestrina's long cooperation with Duke Guglielmo. The format of the Masses provides a clue as to how the problems of the *Gloria* and *Credo* referred to at the start of this chapter could eventually be addressed within solemn celebrations. Ideally, there would be an alternation between a simple form of chant, sung by the congregation led by a cantor, and brief episodes of choral polyphony. The Mantuan Masses successfully combine a nostalgic-romantic effort at pristine simplicity in the chant, searching for an ideal of early church purity, with a state-of-the-art laboratory for fine-crafted counterpoint, itself umbilically linked to the chant ideal. Another example of Palestrina's gift for spiritual-aesthetic synthesis.

Footnotes

(1) Roger Scruton, *The Aesthetics of Music*, Oxford 1997, 333, 340.

(2) Cursory scanning of most of the Masses indicated descending figures in a large minority while more detailed observation of 14 *Credos* in my core sample showed eight with descending figures of some kind.

However, their impact was reduced by brevity on the words *descendit de coelis,* restriction to some voice parts, and non-simultaneity. In any case, to repeat such a device through scores of *Credo* settings would be banalising. The idea of 'descent' is no more than a metaphor for Christ's Incarnation, and significantly it is the latter that Palestrina emphasises in the immediately following *et incarnatus est.*

(3) Knud Jeppesen, *The Style of Palestrina and the Dissonance,* published 1946, reprinted by Dover Publications, New York 2005, 283-287.

(4) Again the idea of 'ascent' is metaphorical. Repeating the process described in (2) above, I found that most of the core sample included ascending phrases but again these were brief, restricted to some voice parts, and mostly non-simultaneous. They followed much greater emphasis on the immediately preceding, more important words *et resurrexit.* So again the audible impact tended to be insignificant.

Chapter 8

Controversies, Choirs, Conductors

Few species of music appear to die out completely. Some go on flourishing indefinitely while others seem to have an ability to retreat and *then* revive, perhaps even several times over, something like the 'long cycles' discussed by some economists. As we explore Palestrina's music it is not enough to probe an intriguing internal structure, a dedicated circling round Catholic Christianity, a cumulation of metaphors, symbols or diverse imaginings. Account must also be taken of vicissitudes, trends and major changes in performance of the music over time.

A striking fact to begin with is that for as long as three centuries or more, with a very few church exceptions, the master's works stayed in limbo, waiting to be rescued initially by scholarly musicologists. Even after accredited publication only a small minority made it into usable score copies, to be performed by small groups of church musicians or early music enthusiasts. Very few were recorded. It was not until the period after 1980, aided by breakthroughs in recording technology, that larger numbers were taken up by leading international choirs and high quality recordings became available.

Choral failings were evident from the outset. An official enquiry in 1565 uncovered a hornet's nest of defects in the supposedly exalted Sistine Chapel choir, and complaints about the quality of the singing there would persist. The practice of including male *castrati* in this choir and in some others would survive, at least at the margin, until a papal decree finally abolished it in the late 19th century. This shamefully contradicted official church condemnation of castration as inhumane. A wider and more persistent injustice was the exclusion of women singers from church music (except in religious houses), at least until the use of operatic styles, particularly in the 18th century, brought prima donnas into solo positions at important points in the Mass.

It is obvious that performance of Palestrina would decline in face of the striking revolutions that swept through Western art music after his time. In the 18th century the 'Palestrina style', or *stile antico* as it was called, still fascinated some connoisseurs. It was a staple subject in dry-as-dust form for learned musicologists and music students. It would echo in small, modified ways in some of the church works of leading composers from Monteverdi through J.S. Bach and Josef Haydn to Anton Bruckner. Bach would elaborately re-interpret, then arrange performance of a whole Palestrina work, the six part *Missa sine Nomine,* using cornets and trombones to make up the numbers, a practice sometimes employed in the composer's own time when voices were unavailable.

Both secular and liturgical performance became rare. By the end of the 18th century the conditions for Richard Taruskin's bitter-sweet prognosis for Palestrina's music were very much in place: a beautiful form of music destined to become a museum piece, to be relegated to a 'cul-de-sac', 'mummification' or 'embalmment' (see chapter 1). But fortunately this did not happen.

REVIVALISTS AND ADMIRING MUSICIANS

In 1788 Johann Wolfgang von Goethe, listening to Palestrina's Holy Week music in the Sistine Chapel, was bowled over. He thought it 'indescribably beautiful', and 'uniquely suited to the antique fittings of the papal chapel and to the group of Michelangelos, the Last Judgement, the prophets and the biblical history'. Some years earlier Charles Burney, the music historian, had been similarly inspired. Their enthusiasm anticipated a 'Palestrina revival' which would draw in leading writers, performers and amateur *cognoscenti,* eventually benefiting both Palestrina and 'early music' in wider terms.

According to an influential connoisseur E.T.A. Hoffmann, writing in 1814, Palestrina's music was full of 'lofty inimitable simplicity', 'pious dignity and strength', 'simple, true, childlike, pious, strong and sturdy'. It was 'the paradigm' of 'the most glorious period of church music (and therefore music in general)'. According to Hoffmann, musical developments after Palestrina's time, though technically superior in some ways, had degenerated into 'elegance', theatricality or mere desires to please.

The revivalists' contentions went further. The vocal and unaccompanied character of Palestrina's music, its *a cappella* status, was exalted. Singing was thought to possess a primordial, universal value, speaking more directly than instruments both *from* and *to* the human spirit. Although texts were necessary, pure choralism and the quality of the music itself could offer pathways to the highest realms. 'Purity', 'seriousness' and 'serenity' were typical terms of praise, also an ethically freighted 'modesty' or 'innocence'. Admirers saw the music's religious focus as indispensable, often in a generalised, not specifically credal or ecclesial sense. They also seem to have warmed to its smooth progressions, modal-diatonic tonality and consonance, though these grounds for appreciation were less explicit.

There were misunderstandings about the music's history, even its basic character. A euphoric book by the music historian Guiseppe Baini, published in 1828, exaggerated the claim that Palestrina's *Missa Papae Marcelli* had in one fell swoop rescued the cause of polyphonic music in the Catholic Church at a time of serious threat to it after the Council of Trent (chapter 2). The revivalists tended to focus in an unbalanced way on Palestrina's Holy Week music. The stately progressions of unadorned chords in the *Stabat Mater* helped to inspire a rhetoric of 'simplicity', while the pathos of the Holy Week music and its solemn ceremonial exerted a strong nostalgic pull. There was an over-identification with chordalism, along with the works devoted to penitence, suffering and sorrow.

In a detailed study, *Palestrina and the German Romantic Imagination*, James Garratt portrays the revival phenomenon across a wide canvas. He shows how Palestrina's music would put enthusiasts in mind of imagined 'golden ages' (classical Athens, the Middle Ages, the Italian Renaissance). Its style would be likened to the paintings of Fra Angelico or the harmony, radiance and clarity of Raphael. As counter-cultural critics of Enlightenment rationalism and its relegation of the sacred, the Palestrina revivalists would castigate recent brands of music as inferior. Operatic and oratorio styles were obvious targets for them, along with much that was showy, trivial or 'kitschy' in church music (1).

Elite circles of singers would contribute to a cult of early music in wider terms. The French choral conductor and music publisher Alexandre Choron founded a school of 'classical and religious music' in Paris in the 1820s. He advocated interpreting Palestrina with *legato*, 'softness, precision, simplicity, much sweetness and tenderness'. The German musicologist Anton Thibaut took a more metaphysical, vaguely theistic view. He described the attic in his house as 'a temple' where he could experience a scripture lesson from Marcello, a sermon from Handel, while 'with Palestrina I worship my God, and our religious language, the religion we practise, is music'.

It is easy to smile in retrospect at the zanier shores of the romanticising. Italians would describe Palestrina as 'the prince of music'. A poem by Victor Hugo exalted him as *'pere de l'harmonie'*, *'un grand fleuve ou boivent les humains'*. The famous dancer Isadora Duncan imagined dancing to his motets. For some Catholic enthusiasts Palestrina's works represented 'the warmest outpourings of a soul longing for heaven' ...'true Catholic music', as opposed to 'the profane attractions of an artistic dictatorship from outside the Church', even viewing it as 'entirely a property of the Catholic Church'. Quasi-canonisation would reach an apotheosis in Pfitzner's opera *Palestrina*, first performed in 1917.

Admiring composers were more reflective. Among them was the young Felix Mendelssohn in the 1820s. Some of Mendelssohn's own works would be influenced by the Palestrinian *stile antico*. An early motet, *Tu es Petrus*, caused his staunchly Protestant sister Fanny to comment that 'this fundamental Catholic text' had alarmed Felix's friends, who 'began to fear that he might have turned Roman Catholic'. In fact, while Mendelssohn remained a Protestant, he went on to contribute to an eclectic mix of Catholic and evangelical ideals in the Berlin *Domchor*, part of a North German Protestant take-up of Palestrina in the early decades of the 19th century (2). Not the first example of the music's ecumenical appeal, nor by any means the last (some Anglican circles would follow with like enthusiasm).

Tchaikovsky warmed to Palestrina at a papal mass performed in Saint Peter's. Busoni would be 'thrilled' by the music and the boys' voices, combined with the architecture and ceremonies, in the Palace Chapel in Vienna. Verdi rated Palestrina alongside Beethoven, venerating him as a sort of grandfather figure. In the case of Brahms the engagement was more practical. He combined analytical study of the music with a response which ran to visual metaphor (chords and modulations 'bursting upon us like dazzling rays of light'). Brahms also tried out Palestrina's and related works in live performances with women's voices. By contrast, however,

Hector Berlioz seems to have been nonplussed by the absence of major/minor tonality and chromaticism in the music, while the lack of drama, vocal soloism and instrumentalism clearly troubled him.

> 'We could agree with the German critics that the music's purity and tranquillity lull one into a state of suspended animation which has a charm of its own. But the charm is in the style, in the harmony itself, and is quite independent of the alleged genius of the composer'. The music 'shows taste and a certain skill ... But genius ! They must be joking'. 'His works are full of formulas and conundrums taken over from the contrapuntalists who preceded him.... Granted that such contrapuntal problems are ingeniously solved: has this anything to do with the expression of religious feeling ?' (3)

Three other leading composers, Franz Liszt, Richard Wagner and Claude Debussy, expressed admiration in significantly different ways, as the following extracts indicate .

> 'The musical diet known to me here {in Rome} is nowhere near as plentiful and substantial as the one I was used to ...with the exception, however, of masses by Palestrina and his school, whose character of divine permanence is fully revealed in the Vatican chapel. The number of choristers is rather restricted; but the acoustic proportions of the chapel are so excellent, and the choir so well placed ...that those 24 – or 30 voices at most – produce a very impressive effect. It is a sonorous incense which carries prayer aloft on its clouds of gold and azure' *(Franz Liszt 4)*.

> 'His {Palestrina's} works and those of his school ...bear in them the flower and highest perfection of Catholic church music: they are written for performance only by human voices. The first step in the decline of true Catholic church music was the introduction of orchestral instruments into it: through this and through their increasingly freer and more independent use, a sensuous element was thrust upon religious expression, thereby severely injuring it ...The virtuosity of the instrumentalists

required eventually the same virtuosity of the singers, and soon secular operatic tastes fully penetrated into the church. Certain religious texts, such as 'Christe eleison', were stamped as standard texts for operatic arias, and well-trained singers were drawn into the churches to sing them according to the fashionable Italian style of the day' (*Richard Wagner 5*).

'You probably are not aware that counterpoint is the most forbidding thing in music. In theirs {Di Lasso's and Palestrina's}, however, it is made to underline the significance of the words of which it brings out incredible depths; and sometimes there are winding melodic lines that recall illuminated manuscripts and ancient murals'. 'The music is extremely pure; its feeling is not conveyed by shrieks of any kind but by melodic arabesques which combine to produce unique melodic harmonies …When one hears such music one wonders how it came about that this beautiful art developed in such an unfortunate manner. Undermined at its roots, it led to the development of the opera' *(Claude Debussy 6)*.

CATHOLIC VICISSITUDES: NURTURE OR NEGLECT ?

For some three centuries Palestrina's music preserved an elevated, albeit narrowly isolated role within the Church. It was still performed by the papal choirs and in other select Catholic places across Europe. But Catholic liturgical music in general would be largely dominated by other musical species. There was much to invite criticism as described earlier in this chapter: not only poorly trained choirs, ragged forms of chant or mediocre imitations of the *stile antico,* but also ephemeral fashions, theatrical soloism and semi-operatic styles.

It would take three developments to bring about a modest Palestrina revival within the Catholic Church. *First,* a complete edition of the accessible opus published between 1882 and 1903, based on original sources and directed by the musicologist Gottfried Haberl, provided a potential basis for regular liturgical use. *Second*, the Cecilian movement, a lay membership organisation of church music enthusiasts (at its strongest in Germany) would campaign long and hard for plainchant, *a cappella* polyphony and the 'Palestrina style'. *Third* came a forward shove from the very top. Under the papacy of Pius X, narrow and repressive as it was both theologically and politically, a *motu proprio* in 1903 marked a turning-point. Stressing the need for 'holiness and beauty' in sacred music, this decreed a reinstated plainchant and commended vocal polyphony, 'which reached its greatest perfection under Pierluigi da Palestrina'. Brand promotion inside the camp could not go higher.

A degree of revival followed in various places across Europe. One was Regensburg, its Gothic cathedral a long established centre of liturgical Palestrina. Another was Dijon cathedral in the interwar years, under the direction of a passionate liturgist and Palestrina devotee, Joseph Samson. In Dublin the playwright and militant Irish nationalist Edward Martyn, quick on the mark, initiated a Palestrina Choir at the Pro-Cathedral, an institution which continues today. At Saint Anne's Catholic cathedral in Leeds Palestrina became something of a staple, similarly in London at the Brompton Oratory and Saint James's Spanish Place. In England many Anglican circles would adopt his music with enthusiasm. A number of cathedral choirs and more especially college chapels in Oxford and Cambridge, benefiting from their long choral traditions, would engage regularly with Palestrina and other Renaissance composers: part of an English *a cappella* renaissance which would become widely admired internationally.

The story of what happened at Westminster Cathedral in London, following its construction in 1901-2 as a centre of Catholic liturgy and culture in Britain, is worth singling out. Richard Terry, a Renaissance music enthusiast, was enlisted to set up a cathedral choir, and this soon established a gold standard of Palestrina performance. A virtually unbroken tradition would follow, relying on some highly accomplished choral directors and a choir school which recruited and trained talented boy choristers, complemented by small groups of adult male professional singers. By the late 20th century the Westminster Cathedral choir, still a fine exemplar of church music, would produce an outstanding series of recordings of Palestrina works.

The subject of Catholic Church music in general lies beyond the scope of this book, but it is worth noting that major upheavals and stresses were emerging by the 1960s. The Second Vatican Council, intent on greater congregational participation, set in train a wholesale retreat from the use of Latin in the liturgy. This move would not necessarily exclude some continued use of plainchant or choral singing of the greatest works of Latin church music, at least in leading places, nor was this the official intention, but by and large it was the outcome. The issue became highly controversial and extreme, polarised positions emerged on both sides.

In more recent years there have been signs of some rebalancing. A vigorous revival of the Sistine Chapel Choir has provided a fillip to top-level performance of the great choral works, with visits to the United States and elsewhere and a striking new recording of the *Missa Papae Marcelli*. A statement by Pope Francis offered a signal of intent. While praising congregational participation in singing and efforts to adapt to diverse peoples and cultures, the pope criticised tendencies towards 'a certain mediocrity, superficiality and banality' in liturgical music. He declared that 'the rich and varied heritage inherited from the past' should be safeguarded and promoted. This aim, it hardly needs saying, would need to include a role for Palestrina. The conditions for it to happen, however, are likely to prove highly exacting (7).

IDEAL FOR THE SINGER ?

As explained in earlier chapters, the starting point for singers has typically been Palestrina's single melodic line with its typical 'conjunctness', rhythmic freedom and pleasing shape. Notes within the optimal range or *tessitura* of each voice part mean that the singer is not pushed too high or too low. She is spared from rapid *tempi*, awkward intervals, tricky key changes. Hence it may be tempting to think of the music as merely relaxing, even dull, and easy to sing.

Tempting, but wrong. For the singer needs careful focus, at the very least in order to deliver lines typically involving (a) subtle differentiation even when they are apparently similar to others', (b) uniquely timed entries and in some cases exits, and (c) free rhythms which repeatedly cut across bar lines and the steady pulse.

Phrases proportional to the singer's breathing capacity improve the chances of *good* singing. Each line stands out in some way within the texture. A sense of 'ownership' of one's line increases. Above all, there is a greater need for sensitivity to each others' parts, awareness of each relationship, an ability to *hear* the other voices. The singer can more readily consider what the other voice parts are doing, which ones she is joining, singing or parting company with at various points, what it is like to sing now with person X, now with person Y. There is a heightened social consciousness, moving from technique to spirit and ethos.

The enjoyability of all this came through in exchanges I had with amateur singers, part of my study. For 40 years a London church choir have sung no less than 65 of Palestrina's Masses and well over 100 of his motets and other works. They referred to advancement of skills in sight reading, pitching, inter-part versatility and one-to-a-part singing, and 'a greater than usual scope for listening to others'. Their experience included 'a sense of unfailing fitness for Sunday worship'; 'music we can nearly always do justice to even at the last minute or on a not-so-good day'; 'a pretty well consistent feeling of fulfilment in the singing' (8).

It may be useful to outline a few examples of what each voice part gets up to, drawn from some representative Palestrina.

First, *the cantus*. In the *Kyrie* of the Mass *Ave Maria a 4* they initiate a catchy lead motive which gets quickly taken up in overlapping *stretto* by the altos. In bars 6-10 they sing a one-off part-syncopated phrase of their own, although a four-quaver ascent in the middle echoes the other parts. A short 'head' they introduce in bar 10 is imitated but variably 'tailed' by the others. Three times they sing a pungent sharp before a cadence. In the *Christe* section they find themselves half-copying the tenors but more elaborately (bar 25 *et seq*), holding onto 1 1/2 breves on a top E (32-33), and rising to F with an eight-quaver run (38-39), and in the second *Kyrie* section they again initiate, this time on a higher register in solemn chant-like form.

The altos have much interest in a fine motet referred to in chapter 4, *Quia vidisti, Thoma*, 'Because you have seen me, Thomas, you have believed, but blessed are those who, without seeing me, will still believe'. They sing through 54 of the 58 bars and initiate a lead motive which influences much of the piece. The word *credidisti* has them singing a vibrant eight quaver run, moving melismatically in parallel with the cantus or reversing roles with the tenors, and uniquely holding onto a final double breve. At one point a nice syncopated phrase occurs (exposed because the cantus singers are briefly sitting out), at another the basses are their companions. In the last three bars, on *crediderunt*, 'they will believe', they sustain a mellow chant-like surety on a single note.

The tenors go on intriguing micro-journeys in a *Song of Songs* motet, *Descendit in hortum nucum*. Though this piece lacks the 'highs' beloved by upper tenors, it gives the mainstream ones plenty of nice things to do. They initiate an octave descent motif which lends thematic body to the motet's first section. They round off the entry phrase with a short athletic figure, by then singing with all other parts, and they go through spasmodic, semi-playful partnerships with basses, then altos, then again basses. Some syllables have them holding on especially long. At one point, with the basses absent, they are exposed as the lowest sounding part. When the 'pomegranates' are hopefully budding in the 'garden' the tenors have a lovely relatively high phrase while singing the only moving part before the final cadence.

Finally, for *the basses*, I turn to a Eucharistic motet, *Caro mea vere est cibus*, 'For my flesh is meat indeed, and my blood is drink indeed ...he that eateth this bread shall live for ever'. Their moves include (a) a starting counter-theme to the cantus and altos, (b) an echoing of the tenors in bars 9-13, with a touch of syncopation, (c) a harmonically vital sharp and flat (13-14), (d) a descent at one point to bottom F (17-22), (e) a plangent imitation of the altos, shifting to minor on E b on *et sanguis meus*, 'and my blood' (24-27), and (f) initiation by a hair's breadth of the final phrase, *vivet in aeternum*, 'will live for ever', ending symbolically on a 1 1/2 breve note. They repeat the same figure at different registers, finally returning with minute symmetry to the original one.

CONDUCTORS AND THE FRONT LINE

I believe that the 'frontline' in choral music - conductors as well as singers - has been unfairly neglected in relation to early music, not least Palestrina's. As one might expect, the conductors I interviewed for this book were inclined to agree. In relation to Palestrina many confessed to initial discouragement or turn-off. A dry-as-dust music in bare score. Recondite or diversionary theories of counterpoint. A surrounding pedagogy they viewed as sterile. 'Abstract stereotyping', 'avoidance tactics needed','how to kill something musical', 'those wretched books'.

The conductors spent most of their time directing church or cathedral choirs or secular ones, in some cases mixtures. None of them were pure Palestrina specialists. Most confessed to extensive sections of his work still beyond their ken. All had recorded some of his works. There was wide agreement on Palestrina's music as specially good for choir training and ensemble. Peter Phillips emphasised the early experience of the internationally celebrated Tallis Scholars in the late 1970s and early 1980s. 'We realised that Palestrina was exactly what we needed to build up good choral technique, focussing on balance, tuning, clarity etc … rather like the challenge of playing Mozart for a pianist …apparently simple and 'artless', but very difficult to do really well' .

As to gender, the conductors were pragmatic on the issue of mixed gender choirs *versus* choirs of boys and men. A typical comment was that women's voices 'add warmth'. As to size of choir, a cathedral format of 20 or 30 singers was singled out as ideal by some, a one-to-a-part consort by a few, with two, three or four singers to a part preferred by most. All these categories had a place, it was generally agreed, according to purpose, acoustic and availability of singers. Attitudes on historical 'authenticity' were nuanced. A subtler and more attainable objective, 'historically informed performance', was thought to be helpful alongside openness to 'one-offness' and imaginative 're-creation'.

In interpreting Palestrina there was general agreement on the need for 'balance' between the voice parts. This could be subverted by an occasional more or less conscious effort to appeal to modern ears by focussing on 'the tune at the top'. With Palestrina's homophony it is natural for a chord's top note to stand out, though even here there is a case for restraint. With his more typical counterpoint a top voice dominance would be distorting. So would an over-representation of the higher voices – for example boy choristers amplified by cathedral acoustics - though this could be just what some listeners want to see as well as hear.

Other performance issues, though seemingly technical, were more controversial. One, relating to pitch, reflects the fact that a typical two-and-a-half octave vocal range in Palestrina's music, part of his 'kindness' to the singer, allows for relative elasticity in pitching.

Hence transposition up or down a few tones is often feasible. In any case pitch has never been an absolute concept. Even a slight transposition, though, can have major impacts on both singers and the overall sound. Some practitioners criticised modern practices as 'going too high'. A few choral groups, keen to avoid top part dominance and to encourage lower sonorities, had lowered their pitches by up to three or four tones, using various combinations of alto, tenor and bass.

Sometimes two sorts of choral strategy were compared. One emphasised holism, a concentric approach aiming primarily at a beautiful total sound, a continuum, 'blend' or convergence of voice parts. The other emphasised clarity of part singing, 'developing the character of each part', 'allowing each to stand out to some extent at appropriate points'. One respondent, Andrew Carwood, confessed, 'I abhor the word 'blending': work with people over a period, encourage them to sing well, then they'll adjust to each other automatically, but explicitly emphasise 'blend' and you risk subordinating the character of an individual or whole voice part.'

The conductors' 'interpretation of interpretations' of the music drew on a wide range of extra-musical categories, as in this book. Examples included ideas of dialectic or synthesis: 'a perfect *balance* of parts', 'clarity of line *and* colour', 'a polyphony *both* differentiated and unified', 'a balance of the horizontal *and* the vertical', 'Palestrina's ability, like Josquin's, to maintain musical energy and momentum but *also* a sense of *stasis*'. Wider interpretations emphasised a social ethos: 'ensemble music *par excellence*', 'everybody feels equally important', 'the wovenness of equal parts as a metaphor for cooperation'.

It is encouraging that a large number of the works have been recorded to a high standard since the 1980s, many for the first time. You will find recordings of about one-half of the 104 Masses - still not enough but a fair cross section. Several of the Masses in my core sample of 32 have been recorded by different choirs, helping one to make comparisons. Fine recordings have been made by leading secular choirs as well as cathedral, church or college chapel choirs. Noticeable are subtle differences in performance style, for example as between Italian, German, French, US or English based renderings. Alternative choral strategies can be found, some leaning towards a relatively seamless unity-in-diversity, others pursuing a voice part differentiated diversity-in-unity. A few recordings outside the mainstream can be enjoyed according to taste, including one-to-a-part, low voice transpositions, all-male, all-female, or inclusion of organ, wind or brass.

Footnotes

(1) James Garratt, *Palestrina and the German Romantic Imagination,* Oxford 2002. The next few paragraphs owe a lot to this intriguing study.

(2) R. Larry Todd, *Mendelssohn, A Life in Music,* Oxford 2003, 180-181

(3) Hector Berlioz, *Memoirs*, trans and ed by David Cairns, Victor Gollancz, London 1969, 182-184.

(4) Franz Lizst, *Selected Letters*, trans and ed Adrian Williams, Clarendon Press, Oxford 1998, 567, 573.

(5) Richard Wagner, in an article published in 1849, reprinted in Richard Wagner, *Samtliche Schriften und Dichtungen,* 6th edition, Leipzig, 1912-14, 11, 254, translated by Lewis Lockwood.

(6) Edward Lockspeiser, *Debussy, His Life and Mind,* Volume 1, 1862-1902, Cassell, London 1962, 82-83.

(7) Pope Francis, Address to International Conference on Sacred Music, 4 March 2017. Doing justice to the 'rich and varied heritage' would necessitate trained professional or amateur choirs in cathedrals or leading churches, improved music education in schools and seminaries, and a role for both simple chant and choral polyphony. It would avoid music that is pat, facile, bare-bones descriptive or militantly triumphalist, or which merely duplicates everyday musical sounds. It would require

sensitivity to symbolisation of divine attributes, including the element of mystery or in theology-speak, the *apophatic*.

(8) This group of singers sang regularly at the church of Our Lady, Saint John's Wood, London, under the direction of the musicologist Claude Crozet.

Chapter 9

Sounding the Mystery: *Sanctus & Benedictus*

Many of Palestrina's *Sanctus* and *Benedictus* sections take us to the highest peaks of his art. The relevant texts are sparse and transcendentally focussed, and these sections come close to the central episodes of the Mass. An exceptional cross-section of Palestrinian style and structure emerges, along with rich potential for symbolisation.

The text of the *Sanctus* has Old Testament origins (Isaiah 6:3). *Sanctus, Sanctus, Sanctus, Dominus Deus Sabaoth, pleni sunt coeli gloria tua, Hosanna in excelsis*. 'Holy, Holy, Holy, Lord God Almighty, Heaven and Earth are full of your glory, Hosanna in the highest'. Under its Hebrew name *Kedusha* it has featured in Jewish worship from ancient times, and the Latin text retains the Hebrew words *Sabaoth* (hosts) and *Hosanna* (save us). The early Christians took over the invocation to form part of the central Eucharistic or thanksgiving prayer, partly as a token of linkage with the Isaiah story of the heavenly choir. The *Sanctus* was recited or sung by congregations, later it was sung by musically trained choirs or schola in the leading churches. It continues to be central in the liturgies of virtually all the mainstream Christian denominations.

Then comes *Benedictus qui venit in nomine Domini, Hosanna in excelsis:* 'Blessed is He who comes in the name of the Lord, Hosanna in the highest'. The back story here is less clear, though church tradition has related the text to *Matthew* 21.9 on Jesus' entry into Jerusalem. In the liturgy the general practice has been to treat the *Benedictus* continuously with the *Sanctus,* as a further anticipation of the central mystery about to be enacted in the Sacrament.

A RIVETING SEQUENCE

Coming soon after the 'busy', 'wordy', tight-packed *Glorias* and *Credos*, the *Sanctus* and *Benedictus* signal a significant change of mood. We move from preparation, teaching and context-setting to an ethos of wonder, awe, amazement. The two sections together, in most cases taking between four and eight minutes, are ideal for purposes of selective listening. They cannot be bettered if time is short and a good sample is the objective. A number from my core sample of 32 Masses stand out. Among four parters, the *Missa Brevis, Aeterna Christi Munera, Ave Maria a 4* and *O Rex Gloriae*. Among more elaborate settings, *Assumpta est Maria, Dum complerentur, Ecce ego Joannes, Missa Papae Marcelli, O Magnum Mysterium, Sicut lilium, Viri Galilei* (1).

As we would expect, Palestrina typically addresses the three *Sanctus* invocations with slow, solemn counterpoint, elongating the syllable 'a'. Writing about the *Missa Papae Marcelli* Richard Taruskin refers to the long phrases on the word *Sanctus* as 'ever increasing spaces' (they lengthen progressively from four to six to eight minims), seeing these as 'magnificently evocative of infinite space'. I agree, although in symbolising infinity verticality also matters, as shown to some degree in the *Missa Papae Marcelli* itself, more so in the *Missa Brevis* with its upward sweeping octaves (see below).

Then comes the clause *Pleni sunt coeli et terra gloria tua*. In roughly one third of Palestrina's whole opus of Masses there are voice part reductions, mostly to low or mid-to-low. The music on *Gloria tua* tends to be rhapsodic in tone, recalling related phrases in the *Magnificat* (chapter 3), the motets for feasts of glory (chapter 4), and the doxology in the *Gloria* (chapter 7). The clause *Hosanna in excelsis* brings decisive moves usually to pulsating rhythms, shorter note values, and full use of voice parts where this has been lacking just recently, and in performance practice often to a slightly faster pace. Sometimes, too, a shift to triple meter. There is a feeling of virtual physical movement or 'inner dancing'. The different voice parts can be heard as connoting the diversities of 'glory' or beauty in the universe or nature.

With *Benedictus qui venit in nomine Domini* comes the biggest change in mood so far. In roughly two thirds of all the Mass settings there is a voice part reduction, mostly to the high or mid-high voices, engendering a closer knit, more intimate feel. There is much lyricism in the elegant interweavingness of the fewer voice parts. This combination can be characterised as intimate, caressing, tender. Finally comes the recapitulation of the *Hosannas,* as described above, producing a further burst of energy, pulsation and *tutti* scoring, interpretable as more affirmation, a series of 'yes's' or 'hurrahs'.

A MINIATURE CLASSIC, THE *MISSA BREVIS*

Not all of Palestrina's *Sanctus* and *Benedictus* sections are beyond reproach. By this stage in the book readers should be ready to consider some possible criticisms. A few settings in my core sample are too short or too long with no great flair to compensate. Some are too tightly formulaic or repetitive to be appropriately reflective. For example, we have probably come to enjoy the jingly lead motive which punctuates the Mass *Tu es Petrus,* but when we get to the *Sanctus* and *Benedictus* this begins to seem intrusive. Earlier on the punchy, exultant antiphonies in *Hodie Christus natus est* have been vivid and exhilarating, but by now they can easily strike one as too schematic and predictable.

A setting with outstanding *Sanctus* and *Benedictus* sections is the *Missa Brevis,* a work from Palestrina's early middle period, first published in 1570. Compact and with a four part format, this setting lies well within the capacity of a mainstream choir and has long been a favourite choice for ordinary Sundays. It is a free-standing Mass with no apparent ties to chant or popular song or to pre-existent polyphonic models.

The iIlustration below shows most of what happens on the single opening word *Sanctus.* Each part has a phrase or two which take the syllable 'a' – and with it the singer's breath - on a stretching journey. First comes a slow, ultra-simple melodic lead of just four notes. Second, there is an upward leap of an octave transacted by the cantus, then the altos, destined to be imitated by the tenors and basses. For Palestrina such an octave leap within a single word and melodic module is quite exceptional. Here it takes each voice part to the top of its optimal range. Then come contrary movements: downward moving passages characterised by quavers, a concave, saucer-like shape and tiny upward-finessing bends. Each voice part tends to return to its starting-point in familiar balancing fashion.

By the end of this first sequence (at bar 17 just over the page), the word *Sanctus* has been sounded 19 times, several times by each part. Full singing advantage has been taken of the open vowel 'a'. The reiterations have been subtly shaded. The word has been given full weight, appropriate for the Most Holy, though without excess. Within the single long phrases the word *Sanctus* gets transported upwards and downwards, both horizontally and vertically, in a way we can readily take as intimating the length and breadth of the sublime. One is tempted to think of the *Koran* speaking of Allah as 'the First and the Last ...the Outward and the Inward'. Phrases from Gerard Manley Hopkins also come to mind: 'first and last, outer and inner, breath and bread', 'world's strand, sway of the sea'.

The rest of the *Sanctus* has almost as much interest. The two invocations, *Dominus Deus Sabaoth* and *Pleni sunt coeli et terra,* feature greater compactness, shallower curve-shapes and rhythmic repetition. The words *gloria tua* fan out in short, graceful curves, alternating 17 times between the parts. The *Hosannas* which follow immediately without a break (another unusual feature) are as usual invigorating. The cantus and tenors hit the top of their comfortable ranges. A clear-cut melodic lead, compressing the one we heard earlier on the word *Sanctus* (though we are unlikely to pick up such a tiny echo) is sung overlappingly 12 times among the four voice parts - in every case with longer and differently shaped tails - combining insistence with multivalence.

Although this *Sanctus* is a difficult act to follow the *Benedictus* does not disappoint. The basses have played a major role in the *Sanctus* but now they bow out. Sinuous, criss-crossing near- but-not-quite imitations offer a delightful example of the genre, typical of Palestrina's *Benedictus* movements. The open vowels 'e' and 'o' are exploited in all their purity, this time with quasi-pictorial effects. The 'e' in *venit* takes long curling quaver lines to work through, which we can take as signifiers of the (repeated, not just one-off) process of the divine mission and repeated 'comings'. The vowel 'o' in *nomine* follows a similar sinuous shape, keeping us waiting expectantly for the crucial word *Domini*.

The *Benedictus* ends, unusually, with its own *Hosanna in excelsis*. For the first time in the two sections there is some homophony with chords sounding through several bars in note-to-syllable minims or semi-breves. But these quickly dissolve into a final phase of *tutti* counterpoint. I will have more to say below about such dissolving chordalism. As usual each voice part has a pivotal moment at some point, albeit usually secreted because so much else is going on. Thus the cantus singers initiate the *Sanctus* sequence, the altos the *gloria tua*, the tenors *Hosanna*, while the basses make a notable series of downward moves on the curving *gloria tua*.

SYMBOLISING THE DEITY

In chapter 5 I referred to a wide range of experiences of music as symbolic. I commented on these experiences as subjective or inter-subjective, their independence of a composer's intentions, their variable forms. The examples I cited related not only to particular works or musical episodes but also to how in a wider sense a leading composers's characteristic style and structure have been experienced as symbolic. I would like to offer a few comments on how Palestrina's music relates in a general way to thoughts about God.

To begin with, his music seems innocent of ideas of war, anger, retribution or punishment, as attributed to God by some religious texts or traditions. It hardly speaks of the conflictual or violent aspects of the God of the Old Testament. The Catholic Church did not encourage such an emphasis, probably Palestrina would have disliked it, and gigantic gestures are alien to him, let alone tumultous or explosive ones. Nor does he excel in emphasising the divine attribute of absolute power and might. In this respect later composers have mobilised 'big bang' resources of singers, instruments and advances in technology, also developing more complex musical structures, for example the fugue as perfected by J.S. Bach. Some of their works have been rightly saluted as symbolising infinity, transcendence or God the Creator.

People who seek intense drama around the events of Christmas, Lent and Easter find attractions in the tonal system which are lacking in such as Palestrina. Major-*versus*-minor tonality can point up contrasts between the joyful and sorrowful episodes of the Church's Year, for example accentuating Christ as Man of grief *and* Christ as triumphant Risen Lord (think of Handel's *Messiah*). On the other hand, as I have argued, there is a strong case for Palestrina's subtle handlings throughout the Christian narrative, his sensitivity to worshippers' needs for stability, and his treatment of the 'glory' themes which stand at a tangent to the 'happy *versus* sad' polarisations.

However, such episode-by-episode comparisons still miss the larger point. They largely ignore the interdependence of doctrines. Their focus on changes, particular events or celebrations neglects continuities and essences, the deeper things which the event narratives are credited with revealing, notably the divine nature as abiding, eternal and unchanging. God is thought to speak through His actions in history as to who or what He *is*. Among these underlying beliefs there are three where Palestrina's symbolic strengths arguably stand out. They relate to the supreme kindness of God, the Trinity, and a surrounding mystery.

As to the divine kindness, contributory concepts are mercy and forgiveness as discussed in chapter 6 in relation to the *Kyrie,* also companionship, reliable support in time of crisis, a personal relationship. If a believer in this divine kindness looks for signs in the music she will find it intimated by the gentle gradations, the avoidance of jagged corners or sharp divisions, the reliability of the steady pulse, and not least by the consonance and the inter-part cordialities.

Which brings us to the doctrine of the Trinity, mainstream Christianity's belief in God as interpersonal, its concept of Three Divine Persons as co-existent and eternal, perfectly distinct, equal and united in love. No doctrine in the whole apparatus is more elusive, indeed mind-boggling. No wonder study, preaching and theology have repeatedly struggled with it. Even the finest Christian art, when seeking to portray the Trinity in visual terms, has often stumbled or gone off the rails. One only has to think of the Father depicted as a bearded patriarch or the misunderstandings caused by exclusively monarchical or male gender stereotypes of God. Compared with all this, does music stand a better chance of symbolising the Trinity ? If so, is Palestrina's music a candidate ?

Attention here has concentrated on specific allusions or local episodes. The Trinity is named in a text, the object of a dedication, a specific feast day or a composer's stated intention. Quantitative criteria have loomed large, with musical gambits around 'threeness' attracting Trinitarian interpretation - the triad or three note chord, or triple time, or three voice parts within polyphony. However, these devices are musically commonplace so that if repeated every time the Trinity was invoked or implied the results would be trivialising. Alternatively, a three phrase musical sequence in some contexts, for example the *Kyrie*, may be saluted as Trinitarian. But this is crude and theologically questionable. To treat the Three Persons as separate in differentiating fashion defies the core doctrine as to their unity or, in theology-speak, their 'mutual indwellingness'.

We can assume that Palestrina was aware of this orthodox understanding and disposed to be careful about it. Hence caution is needed as to a Trinitarian interpretation of his *Kyrie* sections, the final phrases of the *Gloria* or certain points in the *Credo*. In his *Sanctuses* it is doubtful whether the starting invocations are addressed to the Divine Persons one by one. Palestrina uses triple time in the *Hosanna in excelsis* in a large number of his Masses but arguably for aesthetic rather than symbolic reasons. In a few pieces dedicated to the Trinity there is no room for merely numerical devices or differentiations between the Divine Persons (2).

Such considerations aside, once we consider ideas about God's eternal essence alongside basic continuities in the music a defensible analogy appears. Hints of an affinity emerge when a leading theologian, Hans Urs von Balthasar, characterises 'truth' (and by this he means ultimate truth) as 'symphonic' or when some writers apply the term 'polyphonic' to the Trinity. The affinity becomes clearer when the doctrine of the Trinity and essentials in the counterpoint are directly juxtaposed. On the one hand, the Three Persons apprehended as perfectly distinct, perfectly equal and perfectly united in love. On the other hand, the attributes of diversity, equality and cordial mutuality as continuously exhibited in Palestrinian counterpoint (chapter 5). A musical symbolisation of good or ideal community implies a linkage, however imperfect, with a Trinitarian concept of the deity. Hence a tenable claim: that Palestrina's super-amicable counterpoint stands as a stable emblem or intimator of the Trinity as perfect relationship.

Finally, is there a rapport with 'mystery' ? Mainstream Christianity, Judaism and Islam all insist that here on earth God is beyond all ordinary understanding, hidden in a cloud, in the deepest sense unknowable. But although music has a special opportunity to heed this by approaching the deity with appropriate awe and humility, both sophisticated and popular musics repeatedly fail the test. The sacred texts are enveloped within a virtuosic grand design so in a sense it is the music or the composer that 'takes over'. Alternatively, the texts are delivered as if straightforward, unambiguous, matter-of-fact. Even the deepest or most elusive of them are made to sound informational, 'knowing', pat, intelligible, 'in your face'.

Palestrina's counterpoint follows a different path. The texts are centre-of-attention, not woven into enveloping musical structures, however beautiful. Bald description and pure repetition are avoided. Each statement gets repeated with melodic-rhythmic variations, becoming further nuanced as each voice part is enlisted. The restatements do not emerge one-by-one, discretely or separately – rather, they jostle and pile in irregularly on top of each other, and their overlappingness itself brings symbolic implications. It can be heard as search or exploration, diffidence, even hesitation. This is not intentional but one way in which a feature of late 16th century counterpoint can sound to modern ears. There are echoes of Thomas Aquinas commenting on the divine unknowability being such that all we can do is 'stammer out as best we may the sublimities of God', *balbutiendo ut possumus, excelsa Dei resonamus.*

Further factors in Palestrina safeguard against both overbearingness and pat neatness, with favourable implications for mystery. One is his his tempered use of chordalism. Successions of full-choir block chords can easily sound over-emphatic, even pressuring of the listener. But pure homophony in his music seldom delivers a whole clause or continues for more than a few bars (the *Stabat Mater* was an exception). Often his chords are scored only for two or three parts within fuller textures of counterpoint. In full force they tend to act as heralds, flag bearers or points of departure, not continuous features. Significantly, they quickly liquefy, unwind and dissolve into elastic counterpoint, often through mini-cascades of quavers.

A NEGLECTED MASTERPIECE: THE MISSA *VIRI GALILEI*

I would like to finish this chapter with an unfairly neglected work, the *Missa Viri Galilei,* a fairly long six part setting linked with the splendid eponymous motet celebrating Christ's Ascension which I referred to in chapter 4. Publication of the Mass had to wait until 1601. Its *Sanctus* and *Benedictus* sections are intriguingly varied and vivid.

The opening phrases of the *Sanctus* are shown in an adjacent illustration. On the word *Sanctus* three melodic modules proceed more or less simultaneously. This pluralism, and the lack of a single overarching theme, is typical of the Mass as a whole. The two alto parts closely interweave in a semi-canonic duet with a lithe, slightly syncopated motive (points A); the second tenors sing a slow, chant-like horizontal phrase, soon followed by the cantus (points B); and the basses initiate a characteristic line, which is semi-imitated by the first, then by the second tenors (points C). Then *Dominus Deus Sabaoth* starts with snatches of homophony on a brief, nicely syncopated rhythmic phrase (point D). This rhythmic figure soon moves into counterpoint, starting at (E), and it continues for quite a while (not shown in the illustration) with 34 full or partial repetitions.

In *Pleni sunt coeli* comes a thinning-down to four parts SATB, while the *Gloria tua* phrase produces a bonanza of overlapping spiral-like runs, each with seven or eight quavers, one of Palestrina's best. Fluent rapture here leads finally to dense, vigorous counterpoint in an exhilarating *Hosanna in excelcis.*

136 Palestrina For All

Then comes a small gem of a *Benedictus*, most of it shown on a further page.

Sounding the Mystery: Sanctus & Benedictus   137

The melismatic passages on the words *in nomine Domini* build up a sense of anticipation of the coming of the Lord or in another interpretation perhaps they intimate the very nature of His coming. There is a sense of gentle paced, delighted dancing. Prominent here is a plethora of downward runs. The last three bars feature a tiny almost throwaway gesture as the cantus unexpectedly go contra-trend with an *upward* run. The 'name of the Lord' comes across with delicate lightness. And the middle part voice mixture in the counterpoint - shared between the first and second altos and the first and second tenors - results in a mellow, golden, cello-like tone, yet a further beauty within this setting.

Footnotes

(1) In accordance with the criteria I used for my core sample all of these have been recorded to a high standard. In some cases there is a choice of recordings.

(2) Neither triple time nor a defining use of three-part harmony feature in two Palestrina pieces with trinitarian texts. In an offertory intended for the Feast of the Holy Trinity, *Benedictus sit Deus,* the text refers to the Trinity as ever blessed, united and marvellously merciful. In a five-part motet, *O Beata et Gloriosa Trinitas,* the Trinity is celebrated in these terms and acclaimed with alleluias. In neither work are Father, Son and Holy Spirit referred to one by one, thus precluding a separate treatment.

Chapter 10

Peace and Eternity: Agnus Dei

It's all music, the master said, being more than half right,
The disappearance of things
Adding the balance,
*   Dark serenity of acceptance*
Moving as water moves, inside itself and outside itself.

Compassion and cold comfort
*   Take one and let the other lie,*
Remembering how the currents of the Adige
Shattered in sunlight,
Translucent on the near side,
Spun gold on the other (Charles Wright) (1)

The 1580s seem to have been relatively good years for Palestrina. With his new wife Virginia he would have female companionship again and in all likelihood better care at home. The business Virginia had inherited, now turned into a partnership, would involve him in a lot of work in effect as general manager. His canny business sense proved useful, and the sale of furs, skin and leather brought in good profits. This meant that much of the intensely frustrating backlog of unpublished compositions was unblocked. One result was publication of the spiritual madrigals and the *Song of Songs*. Further books of Masses were published in 1582 and 1590, of motets in 1584 and madrigals in 1586 (after the master's death his son Iginio would publish still more Masses in 1594, 1596, 1599, 1600 and 1601). In the period 1581-94 nearly 400 works were published.

Palestrina held the (largely honorific) titles of composer to the papal choir and director of the choir of Saint Peter's. He was a respected member of the Vertuosa Compagnia dei Musici, a kind of mutual help trade union for musicians (ancestor of the present Accademia di Santa Cecilia). Papal patronage would continue after Gregory's death in 1585, albeit more formally. Pope Sixtus V (1585-90), the Franciscan Felice Peretti, would be more autocratic, an energetic builder and rebuilder, though not particularly interested in music. By now, in any case, Palestrina's status in Rome - and by extension across Catholic Europe - was virtually impregnable. There must have been some setbacks and anxieties in these years, but we can only speculate.

By late 1592 the old man, now in his late '60s and in failing health, was thinking of finally retiring to his home town in the *campagna*. He had never lost touch with his family and connections there, and it would have seemed a good place for a peaceful final phase. So he made a surprising move. When the post of organist in the cathedral of Palestrina became vacant, he offered to take it on, at least until a permanent successor could be found. This would mean a return to the relatively humble scene of his childhood, his Mass serving and choirboy days, his period as a rising young musician. We can imagine the old man playing the lute at home or sitting at the organ in the small, dimly lit Romanesque cathedral of San Agapito, enjoying full control of the polyphony in his own hands. But the final move never took place for in early 1594 Palestrina succumbed to a serious illness whose cause is unknown. While preparing to leave Rome he died on 2nd February 1594.

The funeral took place in grand style in old Saint Peter's. The inscription on the coffin was *Musicae Princeps*. A large attendance would have included friends and colleagues, leading Roman figures, senior papal representatives, and of course his widow Virginia, his son Iginio, and probably some of his grandchildren. A memorial service followed. He was buried in the old Saint Peter's (with the sad result that his grave was lost when the basilica was completely rebuilt).

The music for the funeral or memorial service could well have been Palestrina's own *Missa pro Defunctis*. Although an unusual work for him, this is worth some attention. It follows the special format of a Requiem Mass. There is an Introit (beginning 'Eternal rest grant unto them, O Lord, and let perpetual light shine on them'), and an Offertory text which mixes hell and infernal darkness with God's promise to Abraham and references to holy light. Another traditional text is absent, though, one much exploited by later composers of Requiems, the sprawling, part-sinister *Dies Irae*. Perhaps Palestrina thought this was simply too long, although its fiercely punitive elements breathing fire and fury (causing it to be excluded liturgically in recent times) may also have acted as a deterrent.

A key feature of his *Missa pro Defunctis* is its lower sonorities. Two bass parts add weight to the low notes and they take the lead in the *Benedictus*. Add to this dense textures and an absence of melody or rhythm in the close-knit counterpoint, and the outcome is intensely, tightly sombre. The parts seem to huddle together in mourning. Palestrina gives a small, telling twist to the chant-inspired beginning of the *Agnus Dei* section. At the start on '*Agnus*', following normal modal practice, the second note would normally drop a full tone, but with a device known as *musica ficta* he makes it a semitone, a melancholy touch that recurs. The Requiem format means that we end with an exceptional third part to the *Agnus Dei*. This concludes not with *dona nobis pacem* but with the words *dona eis pacem sempiternam*, 'grant them peace through all eternity'.

This Mass is moving and impressive, although it departs from Palestrina's usual handling of texts around reparation, death and Judgement. These avoid extreme dread, anxiety or pathos, tending rather to exude calm, mercy and trust, as we saw in chapter 4.

CONTEXT AND TEXT

Choral music was last heard in the *Sanctus* and *Benedictus*. Their contrasts between invocation, glory moments and gentle intimacy, followed by the rousing *Hosannas,* may still be ringing in our ears. Now the drama focusses increasingly on the altar. The priest has begun the Eucharistic Prayer or Canon of the Mass. He has recited prayers for the Church and those present, and expressed solidarity with Mary and Saints. Then come the solemn words of consecration, elevation of the consecrated elements, remembrances of the Passion, Resurrection and Ascension, and commemoration of the dead. The fraction or breaking of the bread follows. The moment for Communion is imminent. It is at this point that the choir sings the *Agnus Dei*.

Here is the text. *Agnus Dei, qui tollis peccata mundi, miserere nobis. Agnus Dei, qui tollis peccata mundi, miserere nobis. Agnus Dei, qui tollis peccata mundi, dona nobis pacem.* Lamb of God, you who take away the sins of the world, have mercy on us. Lamb of God, you who take away the sins of the world, have mercy on us. Lamb of God, you who take away the sins of the world, grant us peace.

The *Agnus Dei* has a shorter history in the liturgy than the *Sanctus,* having been introduced to the Mass in the seventh century. At first it took the form of a litany with an unspecified number of repetitions of the acclamation to the Lamb of God, answered in each case by a congregational prayer, 'have mercy on us'. Tropes praising Christ in multiple ways were frequently added to the invocation of the Lamb. Later the chant was limited to three acclamations, with the third response changed to *dona nobis pacem*.

Palestrina's *Agnus Dei* sections usually take between four and six minutes to perform: enough for clear declamation, some ritual echoing and a continuity of mood. There are two parts, usually of roughly equal length. The *Agnus Dei 2* sometimes moves to triple time and is often enriched with an additional voice part. In 33 of the 104 Masses Palestrina sub-divides an existing part, very occasionally the cantus, sometimes the altos, mostly the tenors. A relevant consideration here is that many of his adult male altos and tenors would be well able to move slightly up or down in register where necessary. The sub-division allows for two or three-part canons in some cases, mostly concealed within the textures.

The *Agnus Dei* sections do not have to explain, proclaim or narrate, rather they tend to exude a calm, tranquil openness. Palestrina's renderings typically start with a drawn-out two minim syllable 'a' in *Agnus*. These initial phrases are sometimes single voiced, sometimes partnered. The core sample threw up nine single part leads (two cantus, four alto, one tenor, two bass) compared with eleven joint part or chordal ones. Later, long note values and extended, sinuous phrases gather round *miserere, nobis* and *pacem*, including similar prolongations of the 'i', 'o' and 'a'. The section stands on its own with a seamless coherence.

Some *Agnus Dei* settings extract more juice from landmark features already evident in a Mass. For example, a catchy popular song has been emblematic through the *Missa Nasce la gioja,* suitably revamped for liturgical use: by the *Agnus Dei* it seems almost ethereal. At this point the majestic, sweeping curves of the *Missa Ecce ego Joannes* unfold perhaps to their greatest effect.

Similarly with the high voice/low voice contrasts in *Assumpta est Maria*. The *Agnus Dei* in the *Missa Papae Marcelli* comes in at nearly twice the usual length which may seem daunting, but this hardly matters. As in the rest of that setting melody is hardly the point, it is the total sound – the onward sweep of large waves, built on micro-movements - that carries one forward.

AN OUTSTANDING MELODIC CLIMAX

I want to start with the *Agnus Dei* in a particularly beautiful setting, the *Missa Aeterna Christi Munera*. To understand how this works you need to go back to the origins of the whole Mass in an ancient hymn *Aeterna Christi Munera,* familiar in Palestrina's time, with a plainchant origin. The hymn has four short melodic lines, all moving gently in linear steps which echo the plainchant model. The syllabic version is shown below.

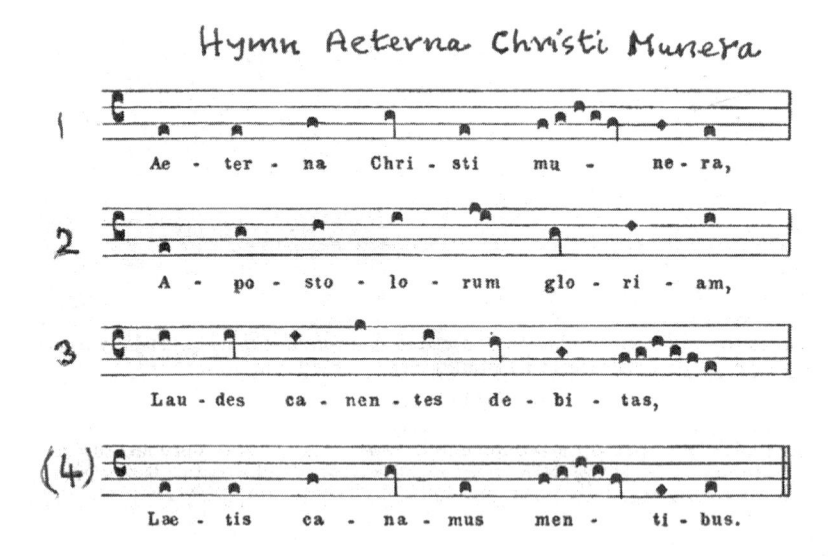

Hymn Aeterna Christi Munera

1. Ae - ter - na Chri - sti mu - ne - ra,
2. A - po - sto - lo - rum glo - ri - am,
3. Lau - des ca - nen - tes de - bi - tas,
(4) Lae - tis ca - na - mus men - ti - bus.

Try humming the notes and you will experience the similarity of the lines and their simplicity. Line 1 is the most important, with its two gentle curves and a balancing return to the original note.

Palestrina has already heavily enlisted lines 1 and 2 of the hymn in earlier sections of the Mass. Line 1 forms the lead motive of *Kyrie 1* and returns much later at the start of the *Sanctus*. Line 2 appears during the *Christe eleison*, then in *Dominus Deus Sabaoth* in the *Gloria*, and yet again in *Pleni sunt coeli* in the *Sanctus*. Part of our enjoyment of the Mass has come from directly or half consciously recognising these simple melodic lines as familiar friends.

In the *Agnus Dei* of the Mass Palestrina carries lines 1, 2 and 3 to extremes of intricacy with exceptionally haunting and beautiful results. *Agnus Dei 1* starts with yet another return to line 1, sung in overlapping sequence by all four parts. For the first time in the whole Mass, though, the line emerges at a slower pace. Minims largely take over from crotchets, signalling a more tranquil mood. The hymn goes on being echoed. Line 2 is sung successively by cantus, basses, tenors, basses again, then altos again, picking up in pace. Then line 3 is sung successively in more or less varied forms by altos, cantus, basses, tenors, then altos again, cantus again, basses again.

By the end of *Agnus Dei 1*, after only 35 bars, we have heard the original lines no less than 16 times. You may be tempted to think of this as wearisome, but the staggered overlaps, different rhythms and melodic variations mean that we are still held within a gentle, far from tightly compulsive frame. It adds up to something of a compressed masterpiece of subtle part-writing.

But there is still more to come. In *Agnus Dei 2* Palestrina extends the four voice parts to five, doubling the tenors and providing scope for more intricate polyphony. Line 1 twice returns at the start, followed by some varied imitative phrases. An intensifying point arrives by bar 11 as the basses sonorously sing line 2, followed by the cantus, then the second tenors, then again by themselves. The final 20 bars, on the phrase *dona nobis pacem*, form a passage of beauty comparable with any in Western music. Two illustrations which follow show this passage, including a keyboard reduction in a form familiar to choral singers.

146 Palestrina For All

Peace and Eternity: Agnus Dei   147

The words *dona nobis pacem* start with a surprise 3-tone chord sung by the cantus, altos and second tenors (notes F, C and A in this version). This is a critical juncture (point A in the score) since the chord seems to bring us near to an ending. It is as if, after much wandering, we are being offered a return ticket to go back home. But there is still some way to go, and Palestrina keeps us in suspense. At point B the altos, first tenors and basses sing a repeat 3-tone chord CAF on *dona nobis pacem*. Then there is yet another 3-tone chord F, C, A on *dona nobis pacem (*point C on the second page). By now the echo effect is almost too much. Having been held in a series of hauntingly near-but-not-quite-final returns, at last we reach back home on a final cadence, starting at point D, and still further echoes, as if stretching to eternity.

'Home' in two senses, it should be said: to the start of the *Agnus Dei* itself and to the start of the whole Mass and indeed to the original hymn. The sequence is sublime.

STRUCTURES AND INSPIRATIONS

In chapter 6 I referred briefly to the contrasts between strong melodic structures and relatively elastic forms in Palestrina's Masses. We looked at the brief melodic-rhythmic leads derived from chant or previous works, his own or other people's, which can be used to start each section and then to form a basis for elaboration. *Aeterna Christi Munera,* as just discussed, strongly exemplifies this category. In other Mass settings, though, Palestrina opts for a more elastic, pluralistic format. A single, dominating, recurring melodic theme is absent. Leading examples are the *Missa Brevis* and the *Missa Papae Marcelli.*

The arguments for a strong melodic structure are obvious. Listeners are likely to enjoy the 'signature tunes'. The sections of a Mass string loosely together, helping towards a quasi-symphonic form, and a degree of disciplined cyclicality is aesthetically and emotionally satisfying, There can be a final 'sealing of the deal' as the *Agnus Dei* returns to first base in the *Kyrie*. But there is also a case for pluralism. Indeed, this may be necessary when five, six or more voice parts are deployed, as is often the case. Then redeployments become more frequent, mediating middle voices more influential. Wholes and parts still balance, but now myriads of intricate sub-layers in the counterpoint can contribute to forward moving waves in the music which – in a satisfying way - are larger and more sweeping. This too can be deeply satisfying.

Evidence gathered from 22 Masses in my core sample showed Palestrina hedging his bets. In seven cases the *Agnus Dei* showed clear thematic linkages with both the *Kyrie* and the *Sanctus*. In five cases there were no such linkages: instead the sections started off differently and each emerged as relatively 'free'. In a further eight cases a melodic lead either lacked defining character in the first place, or got voiced by only one or two parts in parallel with others, or emerged at less prominent points or was otherwise obscured within a surrounding density.

More important, however, is a general characteristic of the *Agnus Dei* sections, namely a breakaway from palpable incident or 'point making', a retreat from narrative, agenda or contrast. The music does not have to 'work' so hard: there is no further need for explanation or excitement, and typically, the pace is somewhat slower. The music favours an atmosphere of relaxedness, tranquillity and reflectiveness (3).

The *Agnus Dei* sections are likely to evoke different responses according to one's beliefs. For Christian worshippers the likeliest pull is towards the consecration and communion. The music's steady pulse anticipates or accompanies the slow procession to the altar. A certain tradition in mystical theology becomes relevant, suggesting a move from a purposive 'meditation', which focusses on a particular idea or event within the Christian story, towards 'contemplation' or a rapt adoration of the divine presence in itself. Meantime the most convinced of agnostics or atheists may think the music 'sounds like heaven' if (or *if only)* such a state existed or were possible. Touches of Dante's vision of paradise - a 'dance of the blessed, 'angels circling as they sing' ? (4). Rivers uniting in a broad estuary opening to a boundless sea ? Water, sunlight and gold as in the poem extract at the start of this chapter, the glow of sunlight on rippling, slow moving, transparent water ? Water moving 'inside and outside itself' ? Two sides to the music, 'translucent on the near side, spun gold on the other' ?'

Not least is scope for a more nuanced encounter with the counterpoint as symbolising good relationships or ideal community. A concentrated listening in the *Agnus Dei* heightens one's sense of this symbolism in two contrasting forms, as suggested in chapter 5. In the highly structured Masses what emerges again is a sense of purposive, friendly dialogue, debate or conversation, in the open-ended ones a sense of companionship as enjoyable purely for itself.

HOVERING AND SUSPENSE

If *Aeterna Christi Munera* brings 'dialogue-type' melodic integration to an inspiring climax in its *Agnus Dei,* the *Viri Galilei* Mass, already praised for its *Sanctus* in chapter 9, shows the advantages of a freer style when it comes to this section. While pluralistic in form and lacking a single overarching theme, it is able to follow a gently flowing continuum which finely expresses the tranquillity and reflectiveness I have suggested as most fitting for the *Agnus Dei*.

The *Agnus Dei 1* in *Viri Galilei* expands from five voices to six. There is an echo of the *Kyrie* and the *Sanctus* in the shape of a slow, horizontal, chant-like line, sung in parallel with closely interweaving curvy melodic lines. This recedes as more or less imitative lines fill up the relatively dense texture. The *Agnus Dei 2* starts with three melodic themes proceeding in parallel. As we get towards the end, within a mere 15 bars, there is a striking fiesta of long quaver runs on *dona nobis pacem,* usually sung at a gentle pace, upward flowing in shape with slight bends on the way. Impetus gathers as the voice parts gambit and infectiously chase each other, sometimes in small teams, sometimes individually. How to interpret the freedom and apparent randomness ? Once again, ideal community in delighted sheer 'being together' form ?

My final example comes from another neglected work, the five-part Mass *O Sacrum Convivium*. In this work Palestrina drew extensively on material in a motet celebrating the Eucharist by the Spanish composer Cristobal de Morales. He showed good taste here for the Morales motet is a finely crafted piece, though he himself wrote a good motet on the very same text. The *O Sacrum Convivium* Mass is a long one, reflecting the importance of the relevant feast day, Corpus Christi. As so often its *Kyrie, Sanctus* and *Benedictus* sections are the best for focussed listening. However, it is the *Agnus Dei* section which proves outstanding for melodic pluralism, total sound and atmospheric.

The opening phrases of *Agnus Dei 1* are shown below. On the words *Agnus Dei* three different lines run mainly in parallel, none of them dominating. A long three note chant-like line, inherited from the *Kyrie* and *Sanctus*, is intoned by the altos, then the cantus; a characterful melodic line is sung by the second tenors, then the basses; and a sinuous one comes from the first tenors. The words *qui tollis peccata mundi* follow two separate lines sung respectively by the first tenors and altos, but a third relatively melodious line soon comes more influentially first from the basses, then the cantus, to be imitated by others. Finally, *miserere nobis* unwinds more slowly with a similar broadly imitative pattern. The multi-layering of melodic lines produces a great sense of richness. Within the space of 34 bars this is a hauntingly beautiful sequence.

In *Agnus Dei 2* the cantus voices first reprise the familiar emblematic chant, but this time more emphatically in ascending shape up to top C, while the other parts gambol and play with syncopations, quaver runs and imitative phrases. There are more three-tiered juxtapositions, finely balanced. However, the most notable feature comes in the final 16 bars on *dona nobis pacem*, shown below.

Peace and Eternity: Agnus Dei   153

As in *Viri Galilei*, dance-like quaver runs take over. Except that here the head motive on *dona nobis pacem* is a small, impish curl. This is repeated 11 times over in staggered fashion by all five parts, a token of infinite peace, giving an almost throwaway feel, suggesting a lightness of being. It is as if, for all his concern for both stability and dynamism, order and freedom, Palestrina in this setting is giving the last word to freedom. Ritual dance, floating balloons, a God of surprises, eternal peace as sheer enjoyment?

Through the whole *Agnus Dei* in this *O Sacrum Convivium* Mass devotion to God is expressed as highly charged and fervent but also tranquil and trusting. For the believer, Christ can be intimated as present and welcoming, the slow procession to the altar to take Communion anticipated or already taking place. For every sort of listener there can be enjoyment in the layered melodiousness, a symbol of inclusive community, an aid to tranquil reflection. Clunky, definitive finality is avoided. The closing effect is indeterminate like a beckoning horizon, leaving us hovering, at once suspended and in suspense.

Footnotes

(1) Charles Wright, *Littlefoot 1*

(2) The broad categories were as follows. (A) *Aeterna Christi Munera, Ascendo ad Patrem, Ave Maria a 4, Dies Sanctificatus, Hodie Christus natus est, Nasce la gioja, Tu es Petrus*. (B) *Assumpta est Maria, Ave Regina Coelorum, Benedicta es, Dum complerentur, Ecce ego Joannes, O Magnum Mysterium, O Rex Gloriae, Pro Defunctis*. (C) *Missa Brevis, Missa Papae Marcelli, O Sacrum Convivium, Sine Nomine a 4, Viri Galilei*.

(3) There are exceptions. Some emblematic features, however attractive earlier on, become questionable when repeated yet again in the *Agnus Dei*. The hard-edged antiphonies in the exultant two choir *Hodie Christus natus est* begin to seem rather overdone, even intrusive. Similarly with the catchy, pert lead motive which has already popped up repeatedly in the *Tu es Petrus* Mass but which by now seems too 'busy' and pressuring.

(4) Dante, *Paradiso*, Canto 14

Peace and Eternity: Agnus Dei   155

Extract from the first edition of *Missa Papae Marcelli*, courtesy of Museo Internazionale e Biblioteca della Musica di Bologna'

Statue of Palestrina, main piazza in Palestrina

Palestrina as a young man, anonymous 16th century portrait, courtesy of Michael d'Andrea, New Jersey

158 Palestrina For All

The Sistine Chapel Choir in its latest incarnation, picture shown here by courtesy of Deutsche Grammophon

Select Bibliography

PRIMARY SOURCES

Andrews, H.K, *An Introduction to the Technique of Palestrina*, London 1958

Baini, Giuseppe, *Memorie storico-critiche della vita e delle opere di Giovanni Pierluigi da Palestrina,* Rome 1828

Barchi, Fabrizio, *Problemi della Vocalita nella Musica del Palestrina*, Fondazione G.P. da Palestrina

Bianchi, Lino, *Giovanni Pierluigi da Palestrina, nella vita, nelle opere, nel suo tempo,* Fondazione G.P. da Palestrina 1995

Boyd, Malcolm, *Palestrina's Style*, Oxford 1973

Cametti, Alberto, *Palestrina,* Milano 1925

Coates, Henry, *Palestrina*, London 1938

Day, T.C. 'Palestrina in History', Columbia University dissertation 1970

Franke, Virginia Mary, *Palestrina's Imitation Masses,* Fondazione G.P. da Palestrina 2007

Garratt, James, *Palestrina and the German Romantic Imagination*, Oxford 2002

Iconografia Palestriniana: Giovanni Pierluigi da Palestrina: immaginini e documenti del suo tempore, A cura di Lino Bianchi e Giancarlo Rostirolla, Libreria Musicale Italiana 1994

Jeppesen, Knud, *The Style of Palestrina and the Dissonance*, published in 1946, reprinted by Dover Publications, New York 2005

Lockwood, Lewis, ed, *Palestrina, Pope Marcellus Mass*, New York 1975

Lockwood, Lewis, and Owens, Jessie Ann, 'Palestrina', in *The New Grove High Renaissance Masters,* London 1984

Marvin, Clara, *Palestrina, A Guide to Research,* London 2002

O'Regan, Noel, 'Palestrina and the Oratory of Santissima Trinita dei Pellegrini', Fondazione GP da Palestrina 1991

O'Regan, Noel, 'Palestrina, A Musician and Composer in the Market Place', *Early Music* 22, 1994, 551-57

O'Regan, Noel, 'Sacred Polychoral Music in Rome 1575-1621, D.Phil thesis, University of Oxford 1988

O'Regan, Noel, 'Secular Latin motets in post-Tridentine Rome', in Richard Rastall, ed, *The Secular Latin Motet in the Renaissance,* Edwin Mellen Press, Lampeter 2010

Owens, Jessie Ann, 'Palestrina at Work', in *Papal Music and Musicians in Late Medieval and Renaissance Rome,* Washington DC 1993

Owens, Jessie Ann, 'Palestrina as Reader, Motets from the Song of Songs', in ed. Dolores Pesce, *Hearing the Motet, Essays in the Motet of the Middle Ages and Renaissance*, Oxford 1977

Pyne, Zoe, *Palestrina: His Life and Times*, London 1922

Raugel, Felix, *Palestrina,* Paris 1930

Roche, Jerome, *Palestrina,* London 1971

Samson, Joseph, *Palestrina ou la Poesie d'Exactitude*, Geneva 1950

Schlotterer, Rheinhold, *Der Konponist Palestrina*, Augsburg 2002

Sharp, Geoffrey B, *Lassus and Palestrina*, London 1972

Taruskin, Richard, *The Oxford History of Western Music*, vol 1, Music from the Earliest Notations to the 16th century, Chapter 16, Oxford 2010

SECONDARY SOURCES

Atlas, Allen W, *Renaissance Music*, W.W. Norton and Company, New York and London 1998

Benjamin, Thomas, *The Craft of Modal Counterpoint*, New York and London 2005

Ditchfield, Simon, *Liturgy, Sanctity and History in Tridentine Italy*, Cambridge 1995

Fenlon, Ian, *Music and Culture in Late Renaissance Italy*, Oxford 2000

Haar, James, *Italian Poetry and Music in the Renaissance 1350-1600*, Berkeley 1986

Howe, Nicholas, ed, *Ceremonial Culture in Pre-Modern Europe*, Notre Dame Indiana 2007

Jeppesen, Knud, *Counterpoint: The Polyphonic Vocal Style of the 16th century*, trans Glen Haydon,, New York 1992

Kite Powell, Jeffrey T, ed, *A Performer's Guide to Renaissance Music*, New York 1994

Klauser, Theodore, *A Short History of the Western Liturgy*, Oxford 1979

McGinness, Frederick J, *Right Thinking and Sacred Oratory in Counter-Reformation Rome*, Princeton 1995

Monson, Craig, 'The Council of Trent revisited', *Journal of the American Musicological Society*, vol 55, no 1, Spring 2002

O'Malley, John W, *Trent: What happened at the Council*, Harvard 2013

O'Regan, Noel, *Institutional Patronage in Post-Tridentine Rome: Music at SS Trinita dei Pellegrini 1559-1650*, London 1995

Index of Works Referred to

Page numbers in bold indicate fuller references

MOTETS AND OTHER WORKS

Adiuro vos	**36**
Ardens est cor meum	**59**
Ave Maria	**39**
Beatus Laurentius	51
Benedictus sit Deus	(fn) 39
Caro mea vere est cibus	120
Descendit in hortum nucum	119
Dilectus meus descendit in hortum	**5-6**
Dum complerentur	**61-64**
Duo ubera tua	**36-37**
Heu mihi Domine	52
Hodie Christus natus est	43, **44**
Improperium	39, **54-55**
Lamentations	1, **53**
Magnificats	**39-41**
Magnificat primi toni	44
Magnificat quarti toni	40
Magnificat tertii toni	**41**
Nigra sum sed formosa	37
O Beata et gloriosa Trinitas	(fn) 138

O Bone Jesu exaudi me	52
Offertories	**39**
O Magnum Mysterium	43, **44-45**
Peccantem me quotidie	52
Quem vidisti pastores	43, **46**
Quia vidisti me, Thoma	60, 119
Sicut cervus	51
Song of Songs	1, **34-35**
Spiritual madrigals	**38**
Stabat Mater	**53-54**
Super flumina Babylonis	**49-50**, 92
Surge illuminare Jerusalem	44, **46**
Tribulationes civitatum	**50-51**, 92
Tu es Pastor ovium	51
Tu est Petrus	51
Valde honorandus	51
Venit Michael	51
Victimae paschali laudes	**59-60**
Viri Galilei	**61**
Vulnerasti cor meum	**36**

MASSES

Aeterna Christi Munera	31, 87, 102, 103, 126, **144-148**
Ascendo ad Patrem	31, 87
Assumpta est Maria	31, 64, 102, 126, 143
Ave Maria a 4	31, 98, 119, 126
Ave Regina Coelorum	13
Benedicta es	31, 32, 79
Confitebor tibi Domine	13
Dies Sanctificatus	31, 87, 88-89
Dum complerentur	61, 99, 126
Ecce ego Joannes	31, 103, 126, 143
Hodie Christus natus est	98, 127
In duplicibus minoribus	**107**
Lauda Sion	13
Laudate Dominum	13

Index of Works Referred to

Missa Brevis	31, 80, **85-86**, 87, 102, 103, 126, **128-130**, 148
Missa Papae Marcelli	3, 4, 17, 31, 32, 80, 98, 101, 102, 103, 104 112, 117, 126, 143, 148
Missa pro defunctis	**141-142**
O Magnum Mysterium	126
O Rex Gloriae	**4-5,** 31, 87, **99**, 102, 126
O Sacrum Convivium	31, 87, 99, **151-154**
Nasce la gioja	30, 143
Pater Noster	13
Sacerdos Magnus	79
Sicut lilium	31, 98, 102, 126
Sine nomine a 4	13, 31, 87
Tu es Petrus	31, 98, 127
Ut re mi fa sol la	79-80
Viri Galilei	31, 32, 61, 88-89, 126, **135-138, 150-151**

Printed in Great Britain
by Amazon